# 1000

of the World's most Astonishing

# FACTS!

W9-BMD-773

First published in Great Britain in 2002 by
Dean, an imprint of Egmont Books Limited,
239 Kensington High Street,
London W8 6SA

Copyright © 2002 Egmont Books Limited

ISBN 0 603 56067 9

1 3 5 7 9 10 8 6 4 2

Printed and bound in the U.A.E.

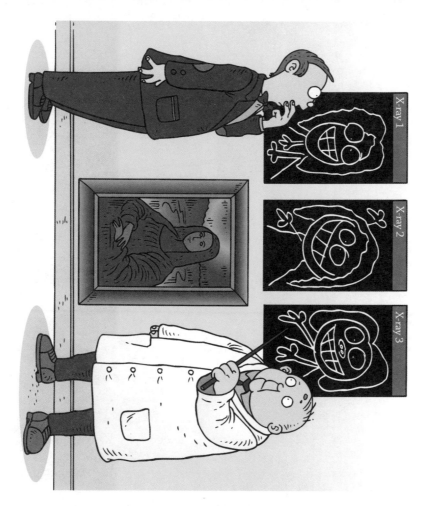

Written and Compiled by: Guy Campbell & Mark Devins

Illustrated by: Paul Moran & Simon Ecob

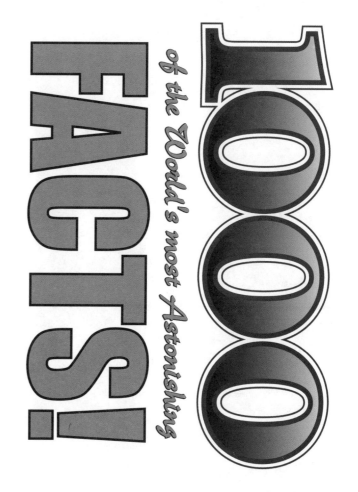

# 1000

## of the World's most Astonishing

# FACTS!

The Seven Dwarfs are Happy, Dopey, Grumpy, Sleepy, Sneezy, Bashful and Doc. But Walt Disney originally had a list of some 50 names and characters to choose from for the movie. Among the dwarfs who didn't make it were Hotsy, Nifty, Shifty, Blabby, Gaspy, Dirty and Awful.

## The French eat more cheese than any other country in the world.

All old wooden-hulled ships had to be kept watertight at the seams. Since dry docks were not available long ago, this had to be done while the boat was afloat. The lowest seam on the hull was called the "devil" and was particularly difficult to reach and dangerous to work on, hence the expression "between the devil and the deep blue sea".

## More people use blue toothbrushes than red ones.

You can't catch a cold by sitting in a draught. The change in temperature may bring on a temporary condition called vasomotor rhinitis, which causes swelling in the tiny blood vessels in the mucus membrane linings of your nose and give you a runny nose, but it is not a cold. A cold is a virus.

## A mole can dig a tunnel 300 feet long in a single night.

The Simpsons is the longest-running animated series ever on TV.

**Blood is thicker than fresh water, but about the same thickness as sea water.**

**The door to 10 Downing Street, home of the British Prime Minister, opens only from the inside.**

William Shakespeare was 46 years old at the time that the King James version of the Bible was written. In Psalms 46, the 46th word from the beginning is "shake" and the 46th word from the end is "spear".

**Human adults breathe about 23,000 times a day.**

Even very clever people use only about one per cent of the possible words in the English language when they talk to each other.

**Ants are social insects and live in colonies which may have as many as half a million individuals.**

Boiling potatoes will not cook any faster by turning up the heat. The water can boil only at 100°C. Turning up the heat will only make more water evaporate as the water turns to steam at this temperature.

**Disney's "Toy Story" broke records in Shanghai, attracting a million moviegoers out of a population of 13 million.**

King Francis I paid Leonardo da Vinci the equivalent of $50,000 for his painting of the Mona Lisa and had it displayed in the Louvre. It has been there ever since except for two years that it was stolen (1911-1913). During the time it was missing, six different Americans paid $300,000 each for fakes they thought were the stolen painting.

221B Baker Street is one of London's most famous addresses. It was, of course, the home of Sherlock Holmes and his companion, Dr Watson. Hundreds of tourists every year still try and find it, but it doesn't exist.

A pound of crisps costs about 200 times more than a pound of potatoes.

**Californian Frank Epperson invented the ice lolly in 1905 when he was eleven years old. He left a glass of pop and a stirrer outside overnight and in the morning discovered them frozen together.**

The first toothbrush with bristles was developed in China in 1498.

**In M&M chocolates, the letters stand for Mars and Murrie, the developers of the sweets in 1941.**

The Atlantic Ocean is saltier than the Pacific Ocean.

**Ostriches are the second fastest animal in the world and can run at 40 miles per hour. They can also maintain this speed for at least 30 minutes.**

At one time in Japan fashionable women painted their teeth black.

**Until 1818 shoes were interchangeable: there was no difference between the right and left shoes. King George IV of England changed this tradition by ordering a set of boots made to fit specific feet.**

Research has determined that three out of every four women wear the wrong size bra.

**Braille was invented by Louis Braille in 1824. He was 15 years old at the time and had been blind since he was three years old.**

Homer Simpson's middle name is Jay.

**A butterfly has 12,000 eyes.**

A can of Spam is opened every four seconds.

**A baby is born every seven seconds.**

As a promotional stunt at a baseball game in 1939, catcher Joe Sprinz tried to catch a baseball dropped from 1,200 feet in the air. He said he could see the ball all the way down, but somehow instead of catching it in his glove, it hit him in the face, cracking his jaw in 12 places.

**Martina Hingis became the youngest ever Wimbledon Champion in 1996, winning the Ladies' doubles with Helena Sukova at the age of 15. Boris Becker was the youngest player to win the Men's singles title, aged 17, in 1985.**

If you could harness the power used by your brain, you could power a ten-watt light bulb.

**Cats will not walk on aluminium foil.**

When cats turn round and round before lying down, this is an instinct left over from the days when they slept in tall grass. The turning action pushed the grass down into a nest.

**When a gas pipeline crossing the California desert springs a leak, the gas companies have an ingenious way of finding out where it is. A chemical is put into the gas that arouses the mating instinct in vultures. The birds congregate around the area. Look for the vultures and you have located the leak.**

**Fishing is the biggest participant sport in the world.**

When Victor Hugo finished writing his book "Les Miserables", he took a holiday. While away, he wrote to his editor in Paris to see how sales were going. His letter read simply, "?". Sales were very good, so his editor replied, "!".

**The first pop video was "Bohemian Rhapsody" by Queen, released in 1975.**

The Walt Disney Company was founded in 1923, and in 1927 Walt came up with the idea for an cartoon mouse called Mortimer. His wife Lillian convinced him to change it to Mickey Mouse.

**Vincent Van Gogh, the world's most valued painter, sold only one painting in his entire life – to his brother, who owned an art gallery. The painting was called "Red Vineyard at Arles."**

In the future it is possible that people will be able to regrow missing arms or legs like a salamander can grow a new tail. Research has shown promising results in getting bone to grow with the application of electricity. Already with children under the age of five who have lost the tip of a finger, complete regrowth has been achieved.

**Every person has a unique tongue print.**

When you laugh, you expel short bursts of air at up to 70 miles per hour.

**Until babies are six months old, they can breathe and swallow at the same time. Adults cannot.**

# Did you know...

...that a cat's hearing is even more sensitive than a dog's?

Turkey is the Christmas dinner of choice these days, but in older times, goose, swan and even peacock were the specialities. A peacock would be served with all its real feathers. Its beak would be covered with real gold leaf and it would be set on fire.

Popular legend states that people born on Christmas Day are extremely lucky in life. They will also never drown or be hanged, and they are unable to see ghosts.

In 1876, when constructing the 550-foot-tall Washington Monument, at the stage when it was 153 feet tall, workers needed to get a rope to the top, but they did not have any sort of scaffolding. They tied a thread to the leg of a pigeon, put him inside the unfinished tower and made a sudden noise. The frightened bird flew up to the top, and out. A string was attached to the thread and pulled to the top, and then a rope was pulled to the top with the string.

Some people in China use live quail in the winter as hand warmers.

There was once a flock of ducks that lived on the roof of a hotel in Memphis, Tennessee, USA, who used to take the hotel lift down to the ground floor when they wished to go anywhere.

There is a wild edible plant called Hernandulcin which is one thousand times sweeter than sugar.

Most people can carry a weight approximately equal to their own. Ants can carry a weight 100 times heavier than themselves.

**Dr. Seuss coined the word 'nerd' in his 1950 book 'If I Ran The Zoo'.**

Ghosts appear in four Shakespearian plays: Julius Caesar, Richard III, Hamlet and Macbeth.

**The name Kodak, invented by George Eastman, means nothing. When he was looking for a good brand name, a friend told him that the letter K was easy to remember, and that five letters is a good length. He took that advice.**

You can buy a large dinosaur skeleton from a professional dinosaur hunter for about £200,000.

**According to some sources, the word "tip" is an acronym which means "To Insure Promptness."**

In most advertisements, including newspapers, the time displayed on a watch is 10:10, so the watch looks as if it is smiling.

**The sentence "the quick brown fox jumps over the lazy dog" uses every letter in the English language.**

Lobsters can live for a hundred years.

**Diamonds have been found in meteorites, but they are so small that they cannot be seen without a microscope. There may be millions of tons of diamond dust in space.**

If you took a glass of water and magnified it until it was as large as the whole Earth, each molecule of water would be about the size of a tennis ball.

**The Sun loses up to a billion kilograms in weight every second.**

Every year, the Moon moves 3.82cm further away from the Earth - about the length of a matchstick.

**Blonds have more hair than dark-haired people.**

Earth is estimated to weigh 6,585,600,000,000,000,000,000 tons.

**There are approximately ten million species of living things on earth, and the number increases every day.**

A person who is lost in the woods and starving can obtain nourishment by chewing on his shoes. Leather has enough nutritional value to sustain life for a short time.

**A pint glass will hold about four million grains of sand.**

Bees may have a true sixth sense, one that people probably do not have: they have magnetic crystals in their abdomens with which they may feel direction relative to the Earth's magnetic field.

**Diamonds are flammable.**

Sound travels at approximately one mile every five seconds (760 miles per hour), depending on the temperature and air density. This is why when you see lightning, and if you count the seconds until you hear the following thunder, the lightning bolt will have been one mile away for every five seconds you count.

In 1845 Boston had a law banning bathing unless you had a doctor's prescription.

**If your skin is laid flat it will cover an area of 18 square feet.**

Male mosquitoes do not bite.

**Bowling used to be played with nine pins. A law was passed in colonial America making "bowling at nine pins" illegal. The potential offenders just switched to using ten pins, thereby keeping their game legal, and ten pins became the norm.**

In 1991, Ferdie Ato Adoboe of Ghana ran the 100 yards in 14 seconds: not a spectacular time, but then he was running backwards.

**Annoyed at people falling asleep during concerts, composer Joseph Haydn wrote the Surprise Symphony, which is mostly slow, quiet and soothing, but has sudden loud bits to catch sneaky nap-takers unawares.**

Avocado trees have been known to collapse under the weight of their fruit.

**Bacteria, the tiniest free-living cells, are so small that a single drop of liquid may contain 50 million of them.**

Before deciding on the name "Sherlock," Arthur Conan Doyle had called his now-famous detective Sherrinford Holmes.

**Before settling on the name of Tiny Tim for his character in "A Christmas Carol", three other names were considered by Charles Dickens. They were Little Larry, Puny Pete, and Small Sam.**

Legendary magician and escapologist Harry Houdini was the first man to fly an aeroplane solo in Australia.

**Author Charles Dickens wrote (and slept) facing north, aligning himself with the poles of the earth.**

The pumpkin has been known to develop roots whose total length reached more than 15 miles.

**The sound of a snore can be as loud as a pneumatic drill.**

Lobster shells and mushrooms are made out of the same thing: chitin.

**The famous Russian ballet dancer Vaslav Nijinsky could jump into the air and cross and uncross his legs ten times before landing.**

Four per cent of the energy put out by a light bulb is light. The rest is heat.

**Candles burn more slowly and evenly with minimum wax drippings if they are placed in the freezer for an hour before using them.**

Castor oil is used as a lubricant in jet planes.

**Swedish people are the biggest users of tomato ketchup in the world.**

More than 45,000 pieces of plastic debris float on every square mile of ocean.

**More than a third of all adults hit their alarm clock's "snooze" button every morning, on average three times before they get up.**

Bug zappers (high voltage cages that attract insects to an ultraviolet light, and then kill them by electrocution) increase the likelihood that mosquitoes will bite you. The light attracts hundreds of insects to the area, but kills only some of them.

**There are an estimated ten billion tons of gold in the oceans. However, the ratio is one part gold to over 83 million parts water, so it is quite difficult to collect.**

A car moving at 60 miles per hour covers 88 feet in one second.

**Skateboards were invented in 1963. Inline skates ("Rollerblades") were available back in the 1930s.**

In Spain the word for hot is "caliente", in France, hot is "chaud", and in Italy, it's "caldo". Therefore, the hot water taps in all these countries are marked with a "C".

The first living creature to orbit the Earth was a Husky named Laika. She was sent into space by Russia in 1957 aboard Sputnik II.

**King Henry V once held a Christmas feast that included carps' tongues, flowers in jelly and roasted dolphin.**

The song, The Twelve Days of Christmas (A Partridge in a Pear Tree), has different words in different countries. In France the gifts include Four Pigs' Trotters and in Scotland, an Arabian Baboon.

**One person in five alive today is Chinese.**

The readers of "Batman Comic" were once given the chance to vote on whether Robin survived being blown up by The Joker. The vote was close, but the hard-hearted readers voted to kill off the Boy Wonder.

**In one of the most unusual military manoeuvres ever, in 1911 King Richard the Lionheart captured the fortress of Acre. The inhabitants were barricaded inside, so King Richard instructed his soldiers to throw 100 beehives over the walls. The people in the fortress surrendered immediately.**

Geese have been known to fly higher than five miles up in the air.

**One out of every 88 births results in twins. One out of every 512,000 births results in quadruplets.**

King Louis XIV of France had 14 personal wigmakers and over 1,000 wigs.

…that the character of Cinderella goes back
to an ancient folk tale from China?

A computer costing a million pounds in 1980 would be sold at approximately £200 today.

**The incredibly inventive Thomas Alva Edison was born in 1847, in Ohio, USA. In all, he held patents for 1,093 different inventions, including the microphone, the film projector and the light bulb. He developed some of the first working batteries and power stations, and worked on the telephone with Scotsman Alexander Graham Bell. He made the first film with sound and invented the record player.**

The tin can was invented in 1810. The tin opener was not invented until 45 years later.

**The Pacific Ocean is very nearly as big as all the other oceans in the world put together. It is also home to the deepest places in the world.**

The loneliest, most remote place in the world is in the Pacific Ocean at 47°30' South - 120° West. This point is 2,575 kilometres from the nearest land.

**Joseph Haydn's Toy Symphony contains parts for actual toys to play.**

During the Second World War, pilot Nicholas Alkemade's airplane was shot down in an air-raid over Germany, forcing him to bail out from more than three miles up, without a parachute. As he fell, his speed accelerated to an estimated 120 miles per hour. He landed in a snow-covered pine forest and was completely uninjured.

The most successful World Cup team is Brazil, who have lifted the trophy four times in '58, '62, '70 and most recently in the USA in 1994.

**Australian Ben Carlin is the only person to really drive round the world. His car turns into a boat, and he completed the drive - including the Atlantic Ocean and all the other wet bits - in 1958.**

Leonardo da Vinci was born in 1452 in Tuscany, Italy. He painted the Mona Lisa - the world's most famous and valuable painting. He also designed canals, cathedrals and castles with central heating. In the 15th century, he made drawings of the helicopter, hovercraft, tank, machine gun, crane, parachute and submarine. None of these would be invented for hundreds of years to come.

**The most accurate clock in the world is made by Hewlett Packard in the USA. It is accurate to within one second every 1.6 million years.**

Approximately one out of every ten people who ever lived are alive today.

**Walt Disney World Resort (in Florida) is 46 square miles, roughly the size of San Francisco.**

When inventor James Hetherington first wore his new invention, the top hat, in London in 1797, it caused quite a stir. He was immediately arrested and thrown in jail because he "appeared on the public highway wearing upon his head a tall structure of shining lustre and calculated to disturb timid people."

Bill Gates, boss of the Microsoft computer company, earned over twelve dollars for each second, day or night, of 1997.

**In just one morning in 1996, Bill Gates earned two billion dollars.**

You can't buy chewing gum in Disney World.

**The loudest sound ever recorded from an animal was produced by a Blue Whale. It is thought that whales can hear each other a hundred miles apart.**

If you could stack up all the copies of the Guinness Book of World Records made just in the year 1985, your pile would reach into outer space. It would be 1,006 miles high.

**If we add up all the time we spend blinking, we spend about half an hour a day or approximately five years of life with our eyes shut, while awake.**

Americans use enough toilet paper in one day to wrap around the world nine times. If it were on one giant roll, they would be unrolling it at the rate of 7,600 miles per hour - roughly mach 10, or ten times the speed of sound.

**A supernova is the most energetic single event known in the Universe. Material is exploded into space at a speed of about 10,000 kilometres per second.**

The word Hamster comes from a German word that means "to hoard".

**Whales have been known to carry around up to one thousand pounds of barnacles attached to their skin.**

The longest period of time that has a name is Para, a Hindu word meaning the length of the life of Brahma. This is said to be 311,040,000,000 years, about 70,000 times the age of the Earth.

**The shortest advert ever on TV was for Frango Sweets: it was less than a quarter of a second long.**

In most cases, if you have two objects, equal in all respects, except that one is white and the other is black, the black one will appear to be smaller.

**There is a chemical called "Scrooge" which is specially designed to smell bad, much like a skunk's smell, but worse. A typical use of Scrooge is to spray it in doorways of unguarded inner city buildings to keep tramps away.**

The skin of a hippopotamus is one and a half inches thick and nearly bulletproof.

**Napoleon was terrified of cats.**

The greatest World Cup footballer of all time was Edson Arantes Di Nascimento, who became known as Pélé. His Brazilian team won three World Cups, though Pélé himself missed one of the finals through injury. He scored twelve goals in finals tournaments, his first against Wales in 1958. Pélé started club football with Santos at just 15 years old, and played for Brazil at 16, when he scored after just ten minutes against Argentina. He scored his first thousand goals in only 909 games. At the end of his career, he played for New York Cosmos in the United States. In his last game, against his old club Santos, he played for both sides during the match.
And he scored, of course.

**The oldest city in Britain is Ripon, which received its original charter in AD 886.**

A balloon released into the jet stream would take two weeks to travel completely around the globe.

**A Boeing 747 airliner holds nearly 60,000 gallons of fuel.**

Snoopy wasn't in the first Peanuts cartoon. He first appeared in the third one.

**All the proceeds earned from James M. Barrie's book "Peter Pan" were left in his will to the Great Ormond Street Hospital for Sick Children in London.**

A baby Blue Whale gains 200 pounds per day while drinking 50 gallons of milk.

**More than half a million trees are required to produce America's Sunday newspapers.**

**A violin is made of about 70 separate pieces of wood.**

A lightning bolt generates temperatures five times hotter than those found at the Sun's surface.

**The average person will take in five pints of water per day. Three pints of that water comes from drinking and two pints comes from food.**

The average person takes 8,000 to 10,000 steps a day and may walk up to 115,000 miles in their lifetime.

**A bolt of lightning travels at about 72 million miles per hour.**

Scientists have determined that human babies are less intelligent that chimpanzee babies.

**The thumb is such an important part of the human body that it has a special section, separate from the area that controls the fingers, reserved for it in the brain.**

Liechtenstein used to have the world's smallest army. There was one soldier. He served his country until his death at age 95.

**In Chicago in 1871, a cow belonging to a Mrs O'Leary kicked over a lantern, starting a fire. Over 10,000 houses were burned down before it was all over.**

Abraham Lincoln's mother died from drinking milk from a cow which, when foraging in the woods, had eaten some poisonous snake root.

A stack of £1 notes one mile high would be worth about £14 million.

**In 1955, a borrowed book was returned to Cambridge University Library. It was 288 years overdue.**

According to a recent survey, 75 per cent of people who play the car radio while driving sing along with it.

**In World War II, it cost the Allies about £150,000 to kill each enemy soldier.**

Cambridge University was established in the year 1209.

**The worldwide, 24-hour-a-day rate of zipper production is 28 miles per hour.**

All of the people on earth weigh about 420 million tons.

**Used car dealers can buy a bottle of "new car smell" to make their second-hand cars smell like new ones.**

In the 15th century, a man was given the title "Official Uncorker of Bottles" by Queen Elizabeth I. A law was passed that stated all bottles found washed up on beaches had to be opened by this man, and no one else, in case they contained sensitive military messages. The penalty for anyone else opening a bottle was death.

**There are about 25,000 people in the world who are at least 100 years old.**

# Did you know...

...that crocodiles are all completely colour blind?

A cat has 32 muscles in each ear.

**At Hancock Secondary School in Mississippi there is actually a McDonalds in the school.**

If you look carefully at the Mona Lisa you may be surprised to discover that she has no eyebrows. It was fashionable in her time to remove them entirely.

**In the days when coins were made of silver or gold, a person could make a good but illegal living from shaving little bits off the edges of coins and selling the precious metal. The ridges, or "milling" around the edges of coins were invented to stop this practice.**

The record for milk production from one cow is 11,756 gallons in one year.

**When a dolphin gives birth, a midwife dolphin often attends. The midwife helps push the baby to the surface for its first breath.**

For some time now, chimpanzees have been taught sign language. Today some of the original learners have taught the language to other chimps, and they have conversations among themselves.

**In research where horses were taught to work light switches, they consistently proved that they preferred a nightlight by turning the switches on after dark.**

When Beethoven was ready to write music, he would start by pouring ice cold water over his head to stimulate his brain.

**It takes light from the Sun 8 minutes and 17 seconds to reach the Earth.**

It would take a car travelling at 100 miles per hour about 30 million years to reach our nearest neighbouring star.

**There are about 30 Lego pieces for every living person on Earth.**

Months that begin with a Sunday will always have a Friday the 13th.

**Forest fires move faster uphill than downhill.**

From the 1850s to the 1880s, the most common cause of death among cowboys was being dragged by a horse while caught in the stirrups.

**The first envelopes with gummed flaps were produced in 1844. In Britain, they were not immediately popular because it was considered to be a serious insult to send your saliva to someone else in the post.**

The professional diamond cutter who had the honour of splitting the world's largest diamond (about 5 inches long) was Jacob Ascher. On the afternoon of February 10, 1908, he cut a groove with another diamond (since only diamonds can cut diamonds) in just the right place, as carefully as he could calculate, then he laid a blade in the groove and tapped on it. When the huge diamond broke, Jacob immediately fainted dead away. When he was later brought round, he was relieved to learn that the diamond had split exactly as he had hoped.

Buckingham Palace has over 600 rooms.

**TYPEWRITER is the longest word that can be made using the letters on only the top row of the keyboard.**

The first couple to be shown in bed together on prime time television were Fred and Wilma Flintstone.

**Each king in a deck of playing cards represents a great king from history. Spades is King David, hearts is Emperor Charlemagne, clubs is Alexander the Great and diamonds is Julius Caesar.**

African Elephants only have four teeth.

**Summer on Uranus lasts for 21 years, and so does winter.**

Although the Angel Falls are much taller than the Niagara Falls, the Niagara Falls are much wider, and they both pour about the same amount of water over their edges - about 2.8 billion litres (748 million gallons) every second.

**The deepest point in the sea is the Mariana Trench off Guam in the Pacific Ocean. It is nearly seven miles deep.**

If you could shoot a gun at the Sun, it would take the bullet 20 years to get there.

**If we were to attempt manned exploration of the nearest star system to Earth with the same kind of rocket that we used to get to the Moon, at its top speed of 25,000 miles per hour, it would take one billion years to arrive at its destination.**

Putting your two fingers up as an insult dates back to the Middle Ages. When archers were caught by their enemies, they had their two fingers cut off so that they couldn't shoot any more arrows. So when an archer was shooting people he would stick his fingers up to say, "Look, I still have them!"

Contrary to the phrase "sweating like a pig", pigs can't actually sweat.

Before the first atomic bomb was tested in the New Mexico desert on July 16, 1945, some of the scientists working on the bomb calculated that there was a three in one million chance that an atomic bomb might melt down the entire Earth. They went ahead and tested it anyway.

Eighty-five per cent of all life on Earth is Plankton.

Polar Bears camouflage themselves more completely during a hunt by covering their black noses with their paws.

**The best cure for hiccups is breathing into a paper bag. This calms your diaphragm by increasing the amount of carbon dioxide in your bloodstream.**

We have four basic tastes. The salt and sweet taste buds are at the tip of the tongue, bitter at the base, and sour along the sides.

**Argon is used to fill the space in most light bulbs. Neon is used in fluorescent signs. Fluorescent lights are filled with mercury gas.**

The Sun is 93 million miles away from us. This is approximately 1/60,000 of a light-year: approximately nine light-minutes. The Moon, at 250,000 miles distance, is 1.25 light-seconds away.
A light-second is 190,259 miles.

**Popeye originally got his strength from garlic, not spinach.**

Nights in the tropics are warm because moist air retains heat well. Desert nights get cold rapidly because dry air does not hold heat to the same degree.

**A computer with the job of issuing traffic citations made a mistake in September 1989 and sent notices to 41,000 residents of Paris, France informing them that they were charged with murder.**

Steel is flammable. If you light steel wool with a match, it will burst into flames and become very hot. When steel rusts, it is the same process as burning. Burning and rusting both occur when the iron in steel reacts with oxygen from the air.

...that the actress who did the voice of the fairy godmother in Disney's "Cinderella" played elephants in "Dumbo" and "The Jungle Book"?

**There are 1,040 islands around Britain, one of which is Bishop's Rock, the smallest island in the world.**

You'll drink about 75,000 litres (20,000 gallons) of water in your lifetime.

**On New Year's Day, 1907, American president Theodore Roosevelt shook hands with 8,513 people.**

In 1657, a Japanese priest set his kimono on fire in Tokyo because he thought it carried bad luck. He was right: the flames spread until over 10,000 buildings were destroyed and 100,000 people had died.

**If you are involved in a car accident, your chances of getting hurt are only one in ten. If you have an accident on a motorcycle, it's nine out of ten.**

In 1949, Jack Wurm, an unemployed man, was aimlessly walking on a California beach when he came across a bottle that had floated up to the beach containing this message: "To avoid confusion, I leave my entire estate to the lucky person who finds this bottle and to my attorney, Barry Cohen, share and share alike. Daisy Alexander, June 20, 1937." It was not a hoax. Mr Wurm received over six million dollars from the Alexander estate.

**Mickey Mouse's birthday is considered to be November 18, 1928, with the debut of "Steamboat Willy".**

Spiders make their silk by excreting a polymer and then stretching it very quickly. This stretching creates single, aligned, crystallized solid molecules.

**Peanuts are one of the ingredients of dynamite.**

Intelligent people have more zinc and copper in their hair.

**A house fly lives only 14 days.**

The Sahara Desert expands at about one kilometre per month.

**The largest iceberg ever recorded was 335km (208 miles) long and 97km (60 miles) wide.**

On average, people can hold their breath for one minute. The world record is seven-and-a-half minutes.

**The human head contains 22 bones.**

In the US, murder is committed most frequently in August.

**Half the world's population is under 25 years of age.**

Water grows 9% bigger as it freezes.

**Teenagers catch colds twice as often as people over the age of 50.**

People with blue eyes are better able to see in the dark.

**Most gold has some copper mixed into it. If it didn't, it would be so soft you could change the shape of coins and jewellery with your bare hands.**

There is no known case of a vegetarian dying of a snake bite in America.

**The wettest spot in the world is located on the island of Kauai. Mount Waialeale consistently records rainfall at the rate of nearly 500 inches per year.**

The world's tallest mountains, the Himalayas, are also the fastest growing. Their growth - about half an inch a year - is caused by the pressure exerted by two of Earth's continental plates (the Eurasian plate and the Indo-Australian plate) pushing against one another.

**A person afflicted with hexadectylism has six fingers or six toes on one or both hands and feet.**

"Rhythms" is the longest English word without any vowels.

**In the Middle Ages, young men and women drew names from a bowl to see who their Valentines would be. They would wear these names on their sleeves for one week. To "wear your heart on your sleeve" now means that it is easy for other people to know how you are feeling.**

It was the Frisbie Pie Company of Bridgeport, Connecticut, whose name - and lightweight pie tins - gave birth to the modern Frisbee.

**Most lipstick contains fish scales.**

The first personal computer, the Apple II, went on sale in 1977.

**A calorie is the amount of heat energy required to raise the temperature of one gram of water by one degree Centigrade.**

**The opposite sides of a dice always add up to seven.**

Our hearts pump about 40 million gallons of blood in a lifetime. Your heart could fill a swimming pool in about 25 days if you had enough blood to spare. At any one time, your body contains just a little more than one gallon of blood.

**47 elephants and dancing bears survived the sinking of the Titanic and got jobs in New York afterwards.**

Flushable toilets were in use in ancient Rome.

**The Cullinan Diamond is the largest gem-quality diamond ever discovered. Found in 1905, the original 3,100 carats were cut to use in making the British Crown Jewels.**

If you stand under an oak tree, you are much more likely to be struck by lightning that if you stand under many other kinds of trees. Why are oaks more dangerous? Their roots go deeper which make a better electrical ground.

**The US post office once issued a postage stamp which showed Christopher Columbus using a telescope. Telescopes had not been invented in 1492.**

Eight per cent of the earth's crust is aluminium.

**One horsepower is the energy required to lift 33,000 pounds one foot in one minute. A real, live horse only delivers about .66 HP. A strong cyclist can deliver one horsepower for about 30 seconds.**

A teaspoon holds 120 drops of water.

**There are now at least 5,000 man-made objects orbiting the earth.**

A pound of gold actually weighs less than a pound of feathers. This is because feathers are measured in "avoirdupois" weight in which there are 16 ounces per pound. Gold, as a precious metal, is measured in "troy" weight which has only 12 ounces in a pound.

**Offered a new pen to write with, 97% of all people will write their own name.**

The average person is about a quarter of an inch taller at night.

## The average person laughs about 15 times a day.

The largest item on any menu in the world is probably the roast camel, sometimes served at Bedouin wedding feasts. The camel is stuffed with a sheep's carcass, which is stuffed with chickens, which are stuffed with fish, which are stuffed with eggs.

**The sandwich is named after the Fourth Earl of Sandwich (1718-92), for whom sandwiches were made so that he could stay at the gambling table without getting up for meals.**

A fingernail or toenail takes about six months to grow from base to tip.

**A sneeze can exceed a speed of 100 mph.**

The Pokemon Trading Cards have been banned from all American and Japanese schools.

**According to acupuncturists, there is a point on the head that you can press to stop you feeling hungry. It is located in the hollow just in front of the flap of the ear.**

Frank Tower was a shipworker who was on the Titanic when it sank, the Empress of Ireland when it sank, and the Lusitania when it sank. He escaped all three times.

McDonalds and Burger King coat their chips in sugar so that they turn golden brown when fried.

**Beards are the fastest growing hairs on the human body. If the average man never trimmed his beard, it would grow to nearly 30 feet long in his lifetime.**

By age 60, most people have lost half of their taste buds.

**The characters of Homer, Marge, Lisa, and Maggie were given the same first names as Simpsons creator Matt Groening's real-life father, mother, and two sisters.**

England's Stonehenge is 1,500 years older than Rome's Colosseum.

**The Eiffel Tower gets a new coat of 300 tons of paint every seven years.**

The estimated weight of the Great Pyramid of Egypt is 6,648,000 tons.

**There are 31,557,600 seconds in a year.**

During World War II, Hitler commissioned Ferdinand Porsche, designer of the Volkswagen Beetle and many other cars, to design the biggest, heaviest tank possible. The tank was completely watertight and so it could cross a river, not by floating, but by driving across the floor of the river, under water. The problem with the design was that it was so heavy it literally demolished the streets and foundations of nearby buildings as it passed, due to its weight and vibration.

# Did you know...

...that a female cod can lay up to ten million eggs in one birth?

Crocodiles kill 2,000 people each year.

**Dr. James Barry qualified as a doctor, joined the army and rose through the ranks to become an Inspector-General. It was only at the time of his death in 1865 that it was discovered he was actually a woman.**

Dr. Seuss pronounced "Seuss" so it rhymed with "rejoice".

**Duffel bags are named after the town of Duffel, Belgium, where they were first made.**

During Abraham Lincoln's campaign for the US presidency, a Democrat named Valentine Tapley from Pike County, Missouri, swore that he would never shave again if Lincoln were to be elected. Tapley kept his word and his chin whiskers went unshaved from November 1860 until he died in 1910, attaining a length of twelve feet, six inches.

**During the time of Peter the Great, any Russian man who had a beard was required to pay a special tax.**

If you multiply any number by 9 you will get a sum of figures which, added together, continually makes 9. For example, all the first multiples of 9, such as 18, 27, 36, 45, 54, 63, add up to 9 (1+8, 2+7 etc).
Each of these numbers multiplied by any number produces the same result; as 8 times 81 are 648, these numbers added together make 18, and 1+8 is 9.
Multiply 648 by itself, the total is 419,904 - the sum of these digits is 27, 2+7 is 9. There are no exceptions to this rule.

**The world's first speed limit regulation was in England in 1903. It was 20 mph.**

When Marie Antoinette, wife of King Louis XI of France, became pregnant, many of the fashionable women of Paris started wearing padding over their stomachs. As the queen's pregnancy developed, the ladies wore thicker and thicker pads. When the young Dauphin (prince) was born, the women's fashions all returned to their normal dimensions.

A mantelpiece is so called because at one time people hung their coats (or mantles) over the fireplace to dry them.

According to a British law passed in 1845, attempting to commit suicide was an offence. The offence was punishable by death.

**According to scientists, gold exists on Mars, Mercury and Venus.**

Where did the word QUIZ come from? It was made up by a theatre manager in Ireland who won a bet with friends by running around one night writing "Quiz" as graffiti all over Dublin. The next day, everyone was asking everyone else, "What is 'Quiz?" The theatre manager had thus introduced a new word into the language, and so won his bet.

**Copies of the Bible and the Koran small enough to fit in a walnut shell have been written by hand.**

Toys 'R' Us Shops in the USA sold 300 million dollars worth of Pokemon merchandise during a single week in August 1999.

For a short time in 1967, the American Typers Association made a new punctuation mark that was a combination of the question mark and an exclamation mark called an "interrobang". It was rarely used and hasn't been seen since.

**For a while Frederic Chopin, the composer and pianist, wore a beard on only one side of his face.**
**He explained that as he sat sideways, the audience saw only one side of him.**

Half the peanuts grown in America are used for peanut butter.

**The phrase "Hat Trick" comes from an old cricket tradition where at one time, if a bowler took three consecutive wickets, he was presented with a hat.**

Iceland consumes more Coca-Cola per head than any other nation.

**In 1935, Jesse Owens set six track and field world records in less than one hour.**

If you ask someone to think of a card, the most common answer is the four of spades.

**In 1963, baseball pitcher Gaylord Perry said publicly, "They'll put a man on the Moon before I hit a home run." On July 20, 1969, four hours after Neil Armstrong set foot on the Moon, Gaylord Perry hit his first, and only, home run.**

The crowd at the Wimbledon Tennis championships eat 27,000 kilograms of English strawberries in a fortnight.

**Stone Age life wasn't all fun and games. Our ancient ancestors wore the skulls of their dead as mementos and ate elephants raw. In the coldest winters, they would smear their bodies with grease to keep warm. They washed with earth, and kept wolves as pets.**

Dick Whittington was a real person. He made a fortune selling cloth, becoming rich enough to lend money to the King of England himself. A Member of Parliament, he did indeed become Lord Mayor of London three times. He also left the City of London a school and a hospital in his will.

**The longest trip in a pedal boat was made by Kenichi Horie in 1988. He went from Hawaii to Japan, a trip of 4,660 miles, and stopped only for more candy floss and ice cream.**

Zorro means "fox" in Spanish.

**A fully grown bear can run as fast as a horse.**

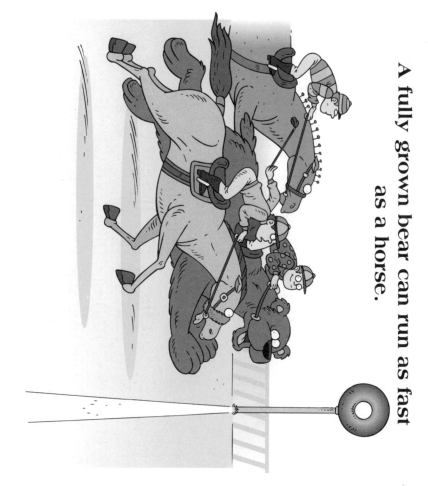

In the marriage ceremony of the ancient Incas of Peru, the couple was considered officially married when they took off their sandals and handed them to each other.

**In the memoirs of Catherine II of Russia, it is recorded that any Russian aristocrat who displeased the queen was forced to squat in the great hall of the palace and to remain in that position for several days, mewing like a cat, clucking like a hen, and pecking his food from the floor.**

There are nearly half a million sauna baths in Finland.

**It takes 60 seconds for blood to make one complete circuit of the human body.**

To play Mickey Mouse at one of Disney's theme parks, you must be under 5 feet 6 inches tall.

**Ancient Native American tribes used an ingenious method to measure the height of a tree or other tall object. Walk away from the tree, stopping every few steps to look back at the tree by putting your head between your legs. When you are at a distance that you can just barely see the top of the tree, make a mark on the ground. Measure the distance from the mark to the bottom of the tree and you will have a surprisingly accurate measurement of the tree's height.**

"Housewarming parties" have their origin in Scotland, where embers from the fireplace of an old home were carried to start the first fire in a new house.

Many years ago in England, pub frequenters had a whistle baked into the rim or handle of their ceramic cups. When they needed a refill, they used the whistle to get some service. "Wet your whistle" is the phrase inspired by this practice.

Men can read smaller print than women, but women can hear better.

**Nearly a quarter of the population of Poland was killed in the Second World War.**

The word "swims" looks the same upside-down in a mirror.

Evidence is mounting which indicates that the dinosaurs disappeared off the earth 66 million years ago due to a catastrophic impact. A huge asteroid, renegade planetoid or rock of some sort smashed into the Earth, creating a huge dust storm and a resulting change in the weather. New evidence suggests it wasn't the first time this had happened. Paleontologists have now found signs in the rocks that another huge impact extinguished thousands of species 200 million years ago.

In one attack, a mosquito can drink one and a half times its own bodyweight in blood.

**In 1968 Liechtenstein held a referendum to ask whether women should be allowed to vote. For the first time, women were allowed to take part. The vote was "No".**

Outer space officially begins at 50 miles above the ground.

**Mozart wrote the music for the song "Twinkle Twinkle, Little Star" when he was only five years old.**

One of the most efficient ways of cleaning your teeth is to chew on a stick.

**Pepsi was originally named Brad's Drink.**

Pigs can cover a mile in 7.5 minutes when running at top speed.

**Pinocchio was made of pine.**

Rain contains vitamin B12.

**Shakespeare was the first to use certain words in print that are now common, including hurry, bump, eyeball and anchovy.**

The act of snapping one's fingers has a name. It is called a fillip.

**Marge Simpson's maiden name was Bouvier.**

Sideburns, the whiskers adorning the side of a man's face, got their name from an American Civil War general, who wore an exaggerated version of the style, shaving only his chin. Interestingly, the man's name was not General Sideburn, but General Ambrose Burnside.

**In 1666 a great fire destroyed 80 per cent of London, but it actually saved thousands of lives. At that time London was still in the grip of an epidemic of "black plague". The fire sterilised much of the city, and spread of the disease was halted.**

# Did you know...

...that a dog's sense of smell is over a hundred times better than ours?

The first automobile race ever seen in the United States was held in Chicago in 1895. The track ran from Chicago to Evanston, Illinois. The winner was J. Frank Duryea, whose average speed was a breakneck seven miles per hour.

**The giraffe has the highest blood pressure of any animal.**

The Greater Dwarf Lemur in Madagascar always gives birth to triplets.

**The Icelandic Parliament is the oldest surviving parliament in the world. It was founded in A.D. 930.**

The hardest bone in the human body is the jawbone.

**It takes 6 to 8 months to make each episode of the Simpsons.**

One of Leonardo da Vinci's less known but very effective inventions was stink bombs mounted on arrows.

**The Shell Oil Company, the huge oil conglomerate, was started by the owner of the Shell Shop in London, England. It was a little shop that sold jewellery boxes decorated with sea shells. He started dealing in oil on the side.**

If you melted down all the Crayola crayons that are manufactured in one year, you could make one giant crayon 37 feet wide and 420 feet long - 120 feet taller than the Statue of Liberty.

**The hundred billionth Crayola crayon to be made was Periwinkle Blue.**

The animal that can last the longest without drinking water is the rat.

**Soldiers arrived to fight the Battle of Marne in World War I not on foot or by military airplane or military vehicle, but by taxi. France took over all the taxi cabs in Paris to get soldiers to the front.**

The dot on top of the letter i is called a tittle.

**The female ants are ones that do all the work.**

The first competition in the world's first Olympic games, 776 B.C., was a foot race. The participants were all male, and they ran in the nude.

**The first non-human to win an Oscar was Mickey Mouse.**

Men's jackets originally buttoned up with the left side overlapping the right so that the clothing will not be in the way when the man had to draw a sword or gun quickly. Women's clothing buttons the other way to make breast feeding easier.

**Every second, two Barbie dolls are sold somewhere in the world.**

More than 30 million Lego blocks were used to construct all the models at the Legoland park in California.

**The world's largest lollipop weighed 1.01 tons (2,220lb 11oz) and was made at Johnson's Confectionery at Darling Harbour, Sydney, Australia on 18-19th August 1990.**

The Jews and the early Christians started the day at sunset. **Christmas Eve means, accordingly, the first part of Christmas Day, and it was only later that it came to be considered as the evening before Christmas. The same goes for New Year's Eve.**

The letter "b" took its present form from a symbol used in Egyptian hieroglyphics to represent a house.

**The longest time a person has been in a coma and woken up is 37 years.**

The Moon is one million times drier than the Gobi Desert, and weighs about 81 billion billion tons.

**The most sensitive finger on the human hand is the index finger.**

The nail on the thumb grows the slowest.

**The term "rookie" comes from the military use of the word. It originated during the American Civil War, when there was a huge influx of new soldiers, i.e. recruits or "reckies".**

Statistics from food research groups show that children eat an average of 62 pounds of pasta each year.

**The world's first form of chocolate was a drink regarded by the Aztecs as the drink of the gods. The drink, "chocolatl" was made from ground cacao beans, a few grains of corn and water and was beaten until it was frothy and cold. Vanilla or honey was sometimes added as extra flavouring.**

One pound of tea can make 300 cups.

**Ernest Vincent Wright wrote a 50,000 word novel called "Gatsby" without any word containing the letter "e".**

At the equator, the Earth spins at about 1,000 miles per hour.

**Canada has more lakes than the rest of the world combined.**

The American Constitution is in the National Archives Building in Washington, D.C. During the day, pages one and four are displayed in a bullet-proof case. The case contains helium to preserve the paper's quality. At night, the pages are lowered into a vault, behind five-ton doors that are designed to withstand a nuclear explosion.

**X-ray technology has shown there are three different versions of the Mona Lisa under the visible one.**

When the Montgolfier brothers' balloon landed after its first flight on June 5, 1783, it was hacked to pieces by the villagers of Lyons, France who believed it was a monster from outer space.

**Woking Council in England held a special meeting to choose a name for their new indoor swimming pool. After much discussion and thought they finally hit on the idea: "Woking Indoor Pool".**

About 3,000 years ago, most Egyptians died by the time they were 30.

**Ancient Egyptians slept on pillows made of stone.**

Russia's Lake Baikal is a mile deep. It also contains more fresh water than any other lake in the world.

**Dr. Samuel A. Mudd was the doctor who looked after Abraham Lincoln's assassin, John Wilkes Booth. The shame of this act gave rise to the expression "his name is mud."**

In the Great Fire of London in 1666, half of London was destroyed but only six people were injured.

**To cook one billion pounds of spaghetti, you would need 2,021,452,000 gallons of water - enough to fill nearly 75,000 Olympic-size swimming pools.**

One billion pounds of spaghetti is about 212,595 miles of 16-ounce packs of spaghetti stacked end-to-end – enough to circle the earth's equator nearly nine times.

The word "dude" was coined by legendary Irish playwright Oscar Wilde and his friends. It is a combination of the words "duds" (meaning clothes) and "attitude".

The word piano is short for pianoforte.

**There is enough fuel in the tank of a jumbo jet to drive an average car around the world four times.**

On average, lightning causes about 83 deaths in the United States each year.

**The most expensive spice is saffron, which comes from the stigma of a crocus flower. A kilo of saffron bought at Harrods would set you back more than £3,000.**

As early as 600 BC in the province of Shanxi, China, people refrigerated food by putting it within blocks of ice in underground pits.

**"The strongest teeth in the world" belong to John Massis of Belgium. He proved this by pulling two Long Island Railroad passenger cars weighing 80 tons along the rails with a rope held on a bit between his teeth.**

The armadillo has as many as 104 teeth.

**The most played song on American radio during the 20th century was "You've Lost That Loving Feeling". The song is the only one in history to be played, in different versions, over 8 million times on the radio. That adds up to about 45 years of continuous play.**

## Some coincidences regarding American Presidents Abraham Lincoln and John F. Kennedy...

President Abraham Lincoln was elected to Congress in 1846. President John F. Kennedy was elected to Congress in 1946.

**Abraham Lincoln was elected President in 1860. John F. Kennedy was elected President in 1960.**

The names Lincoln and Kennedy each contain 7 letters.

**Both Presidents were shot on a Friday.**

Lincoln's secretary was named Kennedy. Kennedy's secretary was named Lincoln.

**Both were followed by Presidents named Johnson.**

Andrew Johnson, who succeeded Lincoln, was born in 1808. Lyndon Johnson, who succeeded Kennedy, was born in 1908.

**John Wilkes Booth, who assassinated Lincoln, was born in 1839. Lee Harvey Oswald, who assassinated Kennedy, was born in 1939.**

Booth ran from a theatre and was caught in a warehouse. Oswald ran from a warehouse and was caught in a theatre.

**And both Booth and Oswald were assassinated before they came to trial.**

# Did you know...

...that in 1983 the United States wanted FIFA to pass a law making soccer goalkeepers wear helmets?

The sound of E.T. walking was made by someone squishing her hands in jelly.

**Playing cards were issued to British pilots in World War 2. If captured, the cards could be soaked in water and unfolded to reveal a map to help them escape.**

Windmills always turn anti-clockwise, except in Ireland.

**The Moscow Circus has a troupe of dancing cows that dance to Russian music and play football.**

Atomic clocks, which use the vibrations of atoms to keep track of the time, are so accurate that they would gain or lose only one second in three million years.

**In the ocean it is totally dark at depths greater than 600 metres. About half the animals found below that depth glow. The light serves to attract prey and mates.**

The human body makes about two million new red blood cells every second.

**When we touch something, we send a message to our brain at 124 mph.**

Our nose is our personal air-conditioning system: it warms cold air, cools hot air and filters impurities.

**In one square inch of our hand we have nine feet of blood vessels, 600 pain sensors, 9,000 nerve endings, 36 heat sensors and 75 pressure sensors.**

The word "macaroni" means "dearest darlings" in Italian.

A procession of caterpillars two miles long and 33 feet wide caused chaos in the Italian town of Fabriano in June 1982. A train slipped off the track when it ran into the bug parade as it crossed the railway line.

The Irish are the biggest tea drinkers in the world, followed by the English in second place and the people of Qatar in third.

**If you could stretch out all of a human's blood vessels, they would be more than long enough to go around the world twice.**

Adolf Hitler started his professional life as a painter and decorator.

**To buy a McDonald's extra value meal in Russia it would cost the average Russian worker one month's pay.**

Russians generally answer the phone by saying, "I'm listening".

**The Chinese are on record as having eaten pasta as early as 5,000 B.C.**

The first American pasta factory was opened in Brooklyn, New York, in 1848, by a Frenchman named Antoine Zerega. Mr Zerega managed the entire operation with just one horse in his basement to power the machinery. To dry his spaghetti, he placed strands of the pasta on the roof to dry in the sunshine.

**The Golden Gate Bridge in San Francisco connects two different areas that, before its construction, were 1,000 miles apart by road.**

**Tasmania, Australia has the cleanest air in the inhabited world.**

Hans Christian Andersen, creator of numerous famous fairy tales, was word-blind. He never learned to spell correctly, and his publishers always had the spelling errors corrected.

**The doll Barbie's full name is "Barbie Millicent Roberts."**

President John F. Kennedy could read four newspapers in 20 minutes.

**Walt Disney was afraid of mice.**

Anne Boleyn, Queen Elizabeth I's mother, had six fingers on one hand.

**Pop star Sheryl Crow's front two teeth are false - she had them knocked out when she tripped on the stage early in her career.**

There is a tea in China called "white tea". It is simply boiled water.

**A Positive Giant is a lightning strike that hits the ground up to 20 miles away from the thunderstorm. Because it seems to strike from a storm-free sky it is known as "A Bolt From The Blue". These "Positive Giant" flashes strike between the storm's top and the Earth and carry many times the destructive energy of a normal strike.**

In Taiwan, the Pepsi-Cola slogan "Come Alive with the Pepsi Generation" was reportedly translated on posters as "Pepsi brings your ancestors back from the dead".

In the average lifetime, a person will walk the equivalent of five times around the equator.

**When you sneeze, all your bodily functions stop, even your heart.**

The 57 on Heinz Ketchup bottles represents the number of varieties of pickles the company once sold.

**The asteroid that is believed to have caused the extinction of the dinosaurs was named Chixalub.**

From 1974 to 1976, a young man in Taiwan wrote 700 love letters to his girlfriend, trying to talk her into marriage. He succeeded—she married the postman who delivered her letters.

**Because it has no backbone, a 70-pound octopus could squeeze through a hole the size of a tennis ball.**

Ancient Egyptians kept dogs for their looks as well as for hunting. Vases depicting the beautiful Afghan hound have been unearthed that date back to 4,000 BC.

The heaviest breed of dog is the Saint Bernard, which can tip the scales at up to 150 kilos (around 300 pounds).

In 1945, a foxhound called Lena gave birth to a litter of 23 puppies.

A Mexican restaurant in San Francisco offered a lifetime of free lunches to anyone willing to get a tattoo of its logo, "Jimmy the Corn Man", a sombrero-wearing boy riding a blazing corncob. Amazingly, 38 people have braved the needle in return for a permanent coupon at Casa Sanchez so far.

Ruth Clarke, 23, of London, underwent surgery to correct a lifelong breathing problem in 1981. She was presented with a tiddlywink, which doctors had removed from her nose. The wink had been in her nose since she put it up there as a toddler.

In 1989, an American weapons company ran a "Scratch and Sniff" advertisement in the Armed Forces Journal. It pictured two battling helicopters, and when part of the ad was scratched, it gave off the smell of cordite, the odour left in the air after a rocket explosion.

"Jenga" is a Swahili word that means "to build."

Mr Potato Head was the first toy product ever advertised on television.

# Did you know...

...that giraffes, despite having very long necks, don't have any vocal chords?

The first cartoon hero to be turned into a film was Zorro. The masked swordsman made his first appearance in "The Mark of Zorro" in 1920, just one year after the comic was launched.

The only player ever to score a hat-trick in a World Cup Final was England's Geoff Hurst, now Sir Geoff, who knocked three in against Germany in 1966.

The longest Scalextric trip was non-stop for 866 hours 44 minutes, covering 2,850 kilometres. It was done by a model Jaguar in Southbourne, Dorset.

Stuntman Dick Sheppard of Gloucester crashed over 2,000 cars in the course of his job from 1951 to 1993.

Artist and scientist Leonardo da Vinci was interested in biology and secretly chopped up 30 dead human bodies to draw them and see how they worked.

The first hot air balloon and the first parachute were both invented in France, in the same year.

Islands come and go all the time. The world's newest island, called Metis Shoal, is in the Ha'apai group, part of Tonga. It was first spotted on June 6th, 1995. It popped up due to some heavy activity from underwater volcanoes.

The word "Tonka" means "great" in the Native American language of Sioux.

In 1933 Mickey Mouse received 800,000 fan letters.

**98% of Japanese people are cremated when they die, to save space.**

The biggest ship in the world is an oil tanker called Jahre Viking. It is 458.5 metres long and it weighs 564,763 tonnes.

**Richard Branson left school at 16. Now he has his own airline and railway.**

The longest-running comic strip still being drawn is "The Katzenjammer Kids". Created by Rudolph Dirks and first published 1897, the kids are still published in 50 newspapers. They are now drawn by cartoonist Hy Eisman.

**A single colour animation cell from the 1937 Walt Disney classic, "Snow White", sold in 1991 for £115,000.**

The animators of the film "Chicken Run" used 2,380 kg (5,247 lb) of Plasticine.

**In Disney's "Fantasia", the Sorcerer's name is "Yensid" which is Disney spelt backwards.**

Walt Disney's autograph bears no resemblance to the famous Disney logo.

**It was illegal to sell ET dolls in France because there is a law against selling dolls without human faces.**

A dog can hear sounds that are 100 times fainter than the faintest sounds that a human can hear. If a person can just hear a noise that is coming from ten feet away, a dog could hear that same noise from 100 feet away.

Clans long ago that wanted to get rid of their unwanted people without killing them, used to burn down their houses. This is where we get the expression "he got fired".

The Teddy Bear got its name from American President Theodore ("Teddy") Roosevelt.

Astronauts of the Apollo 8 mission carried Silly Putty into space with them to help fasten down tools during weightlessness.

Pinocchio is Italian for "pine eyes".

The movie playing at the drive-in cinema at the beginning of "The Flintstones" is "The Monster".

Babies are born without knee caps. They don't appear until the child reaches two to six years of age.

1816 has been called the "Year Without Summer", because Canada and the northeastern USA experienced cold and snow throughout the summer months. Dust from a volcano eruption in the Dutch East Indies blocked part of the sun's warmth.

There are approximately ten million bricks in the Empire State Building.

The lightning that we see goes from the ground to the sky in what is known as the "return stroke" at one third of the speed of light. We can't see the initial "stepped leader" that passes from the sky to the ground.

The king of hearts is the only king without a moustache.

**There is about a quarter of a pound of salt in every gallon of seawater.**

The state of Florida is bigger than England.

**Owls are some of the very few birds who can see the colour blue.**

In Chinese, the Kentucky Fried Chicken slogan "finger-lickin' good" was translated as "eat your fingers off".

**All of the roles in Shakespeare's plays were originally acted by men and boys. In England at that time, it wasn't considered proper for females to appear on stage.**

The Wright Brothers tested the first aeroplane in a wind tunnel before flying it.

**Air-filled tyres were used on bicycles before they were used on motorcars.**

In 1913, a Russian airline became the first to introduce a toilet on board.

**In 1620, Dutch inventor Cornelius van Drebbel launched the world's first submarine in the Thames.**

Over 2,500 left-handed people a year are killed from using products made for right-handed people.

**Legendary artist Pablo Picasso left 13,500 paintings, 100,000 prints and engravings, 34,000 book illustrations and 300 works of sculpture and ceramics.**

In the 1990s a hunter in Uganda was sought by local authorities for illegally hunting gorillas. He was shooting them with a tranquillizer gun and dressing them in clown suits. Six adult gorillas were found wandering around in this condition. A spokesman for the authorities stated they felt this was a cruel practice, since they had to tranquillize the gorillas again to take the suits off.

**In October 2000, a Sicilian cat called Fufu ran away from home after her family brought a new pet dog into the house. Some time later, the dog passed away. The day after the dog's death, Fufu returned home with a new mate and three kittens, a full eight years after she had first disappeared on the dog's arrival.**

**The people killed most often during bank robberies are the robbers.**

British soldiers were nicknamed "Tommies" in World War 1 because the example name on forms for becoming a soldier was Thomas Atkins. (The example name on American forms is John Smith.) British sailors were nicknamed "Limeys" by 18th-century Americans because of the limes they ate on board ship during long sea journeys to combat scurvy, a medical complaint brought on by lack of vitamin C.

**Napoleon carried chocolate on all his military campaigns.**

The pilot with the most flying hours is American John Edward Long. From May 1933 to April 1977 he flew 62,654 hours, achieving a total of more than seven years airborne.

**Milk chocolate was invented by Daniel Peter, who sold the concept to his neighbour Henri Nestlé.**

The world's oldest existing restaurant opened in Kai-Feng, China in 1153.

**Wine is sold in tinted bottles because it spoils when exposed to light.**

The shortest British monarch was Charles I, who was 4 feet, 9 inches tall.

**It takes the human eyes about an hour to adapt completely to seeing in the near dark. Once they have adapted, however, the eyes are about 100,000 times more sensitive to light than they are during daylight hours.**

The first parachute jump from an aeroplane was made by Captain Berry at St. Louis, Missouri, in 1912.

**Tourism is the world's biggest industry, affecting 240 million jobs.**

Radio waves travel so much faster than sound waves that a broadcast voice will be heard 10,000 miles away sooner than it will in the back of the room in which it is being recorded.

**On the Pacific island of Chuuk, local boys can make beautiful girls fall in love with them using a potion made from centipedes' teeth and stingrays' tails.**

The first movie to use sound was "The Jazz Singer," released in 1927. The first words, spoken by Al Jolson, were: "Wait a minute, you ain't heard nothing yet."

**The Bank of Vernal, in Vernal, Utah is the only bank in the world that was built from bricks sent through the post. In 1919 the builders realized that it was cheaper to send the bricks through the United States Postal System (seven bricks to a package) than to have them shipped commercially from Salt Lake City.**

Two hundred and twenty-six soldiers lost their lives in 1850 when they crossed a suspension bridge that spanned the Maine at Angers, France. They were all marching in step and had caused an increased resonance (vibration) to the bridge. Ever since this episode, troops all over the world are ordered to break step (march out of step) when crossing a bridge.

# Did you know…

…that the New York Times of the 14th September, 1987 had 1,612 pages and weighed twelve pounds?

On average, a movie makes about five times as much money from its video sales and rental than from its cinema takings.

**The movie with the biggest cast ever was the 1982 British movie "Gandhi". It featured 300,000 people.**

Elvis Presley was an avid gun collector. His collection of 40 weapons included M-16s and a Thompson sub-machine gun.

**Ireland has won the most Eurovision song contests (seven times).**

The famous white Hollywood sign near Los Angeles was first erected in 1923. It was a property sales advertisement, and originally read "Hollywoodland".

**Frenchman Michel Lotito has a very unusual diet. Born on June 15, 1950, he has been consuming large quantities of metal and glass since he was nine years old. To date, he has eaten supermarket carts, television sets, bicycles, chandeliers, razor blades, bullets, nuts and bolts, lengths of chain, computers, and an entire Cessna 150 light aircraft, which took him nearly two years to consume.**

Robots exist equipped with arms, tools, and a video camera, that can carry out surgery while the surgeon watches on a screen and directs the robot using a computer. The surgeon doesn't even have to be in the same room, or the same country.

**Leather money was used in Russia right up until the 17th century.**

In 1932, when a shortage of cash occurred in Tenino, Washington, USA, banknotes were made out of wood.

**In 1894, there were only four cars in America.**

The side of a hammer is called the "cheek".

**The song "Happy Birthday to You" was originally written by sisters Mildred and Patty Hill as "Good Morning to You." The words were changed and it was published in 1935.**

Ten inches of snow contains the same amount of water as one inch of rain.

**Bats are more closely related to humans than they are to rats.**

Glass is not a solid. Made of sand and other substances, glass is what scientists call a "supercooled liquid".

**Pieces of bread were used to erase lead pencil before rubber came into use.**

In Fairfield, Montana, over the course of twelve hours on December 24, 1924, the temperature dropped 84 degrees. It was 63 degrees Fahrenheit at noon, falling to -21 degrees by midnight.

**You can make edible cheese from the milk of 24 different mammals.**

When the Titanic sank there was 7,500 lbs of ham on it.

**December 25 was not celebrated as the birth date of Jesus until the year A.D. 440.**

**The lowest temperature ever recorded in the world was 129 degrees below zero at Vostok, Antarctica, on July 21, 1983.**

The 20 million Mexican Free-tailed Bats that live in Bracken Cave in Texas eat 250 tons of insects every night.

**A dog in Bangkok says "bahk-bahk".**

"Duffer" is Australian slang for a cattle thief.

**A law passed in Nebraska in 1912 really made life difficult for drivers. In the country at night they were required to stop every 150 yards, send up a skyrocket, then wait eight minutes for the road to clear before proceeding cautiously, all the while blowing their horn and shooting off flares.**

A newborn baby expels its own body weight in poo every 60 hours.

**A person swallows approximately 295 times while eating dinner.**

On average, a person chews a piece of gum 5,500 times before spitting it out.

**A scorpion could survive for three weeks if it was embedded in a block of ice.**

A square foot of lawn has about 3,000 blades of grass in it. A square foot of fairway on a golf course has 4,500, and on a putting green there are close to 8,000.

**Mosquito repellents don't actually repel. They hide you. The spray blocks the mosquito's sensors so they don't know you are there.**

The subject of the first printed book in England was chess.

**If it was possible for the human voice to be carried naturally for great distances through the air, it would take 14 hours for a shout bellowed in Australia to be heard on the west coast of the USA.**

The American showman known as General Tom Thumb was only 102cm (3ft 4ins) tall when he died in 1885.

**A teaspoonful of neutron star material weighs about 10 million tons.**

Scientists at Oxford University's Imperial Cancer Research Fund found that people who eat fresh fruit daily had 24 per cent fewer heart attacks than people who don't.

**A newborn turkey chick has to be taught to eat, or it will starve.**

The highest point of the Earth, with an elevation of 29,141 feet, is the top of Mount Everest in Tibet.

A toothpick is the object most often choked on by Americans.

According to tests made at the Institute for the Study of Animal Problems in Washington, D.C., dogs and cats, like people, are either right-handed or left-handed - that is, they prefer to use either their right or left paws.

Two out of five women in America dye their hair.

Before 1859, baseball umpires sat behind the batter in rocking chairs.

Before American football players venture on to the field, they put on about 13 pounds of protective clothing.

A stretched-out Slinky toy is 87 feet long.

The world consumes one billion gallons of petroleum a day.

There is no wind on the moon, so, unless someone disturbs them, an astronaut's footprints will last forever.

More than 100 descendants of Johann Sebastian Bach have been cathedral organists.

Richard the Lionheart (Richard I of England), spent more than 95 per cent of his reign on foreign shores. He visited England only twice.

**The six official languages of the United Nations are: English, French, Arabic, Chinese, Russian and Spanish.**

Before 1850, golf balls were made of leather and stuffed with feathers.

**Eggs are sold on bits of string in Korea.**

If you ate too many carrots you would actually turn orange.

**In a normal lifetime, an American will eat 200 pounds of peanuts.**

In old England, when customers got unruly, the pub landlord would tell them to mind their own pints and quarts and settle down. It's where we get the phrase "Mind your P's and Q's".

**Rubber is an important ingredient in the manufacture of bubble-gum.**

The cone-shaped dunce's cap, once used in the classroom, originates from a paper cone that was placed on the heads of accused witches during the Middle Ages.

**Men spend about 106 days out of their lives shaving.**

The human tongue tastes bitter things with the taste buds at the back. Salty flavours are tasted in the middle of the tongue, and sweet flavours at the tip.

**If you put a raisin in a glass of champagne, it will keep floating to the top and sinking to the bottom until the champagne has gone flat.**

The expression "tit for tat" comes from "dit vor dat" meaning "this for that" in Dutch.

**The name "Jeep" came from the abbreviation used in the army for the General Purpose vehicle, G.P.**

The biggest tree in the world is "General Sherman", a Giant Sequoia in California - 83 metres tall and 25 metres round.

**Ambulances were developed by Napoleon's surgeon in his Italian campaign of 1796-97.**

Actor Keanu Reeve's first name means "cool breeze over the mountains" in the Hawaiian language.

**The Italian flag was designed by Napoleon Bonaparte.**

You are born with 300 bones, but by the time you reach adulthood, you have only 206.

**It requires the use of 72 muscles to speak a single word.**

Adolf Hitler was fascinated by hands. In his library there was a well-thumbed book containing pictures and drawings of hands belonging to famous people throughout history. He liked particularly to show his guests how closely his own hands resembled those of Frederick the Great, one of his heroes.

**Bananas don't grow on trees, but on "rhizomes".**

# Did you know...

...that sharks are immune to every known disease and they never get ill?

A housewife from Prague, Vera Czermak, jumped out of her third-floor window when she found out her husband had been unfaithful. She recovered in hospital after landing on her husband, who was killed.

**Legend has it that an itchy nose indicates that its owner is about to be either kissed or cursed, will run into a gatepost or shake hands with a fool.**

Mentioning pigs is bad luck at sea.

**A law during the reign of Queen Elizabeth I declared that any woman who, through the use of false hair, make-up, high-heeled shoes or other devices, led a man into marriage, could be punished as a witch.**

In 1063, the River Thames froze over for 14 weeks.

**King Kokodo of the Congo ruled for three years after his death. His body was moved around in a square coffin on wheels while he made up his mind whether to stay dead or not. He decided to stay dead.**

In March 1983, West German police arrested an Austrian tramp for cooking his onion soup over the eternal flame at Berlin's war memorial.

**In ancient China, towns were often arranged in patterns so that if seen from the air the whole community would resemble an animal or a symbolic design. Some were arranged to look like snakes, stars, sunbursts or dragons.**

**The amount of water on Earth has remained the same since the planet was created some 4,600 million years ago.**

Table tennis was first played with balls made from champagne corks and bats made from cigar-box lids.

**The world's biggest forest is in Siberia. It covers over 17 million square kilometres.**

There are more than 14,000 types of rice.

**Cornish pasties were the staple diet of Cornish miners about 150 years ago. Each pasty was marked with the owner's initials at one end. The hungry man would always start at the other, so that if he could not eat it all at once, it still had his mark on when he went back to claim it later.**

The most difficult tongue-twister is "The sixth sick sheik's sixth sheep's sick".

**The world's oldest piece of chewing gum is over 9,000 years old.**

Norway is called "the land of the midnight sun" because in the north, the Sun does not set from May until the end of July.

**It took 214 crates to transport the Statue of Liberty from France to New York in 1885.**

The beam of light shining from the top of the Luxor hotel and casino in Las Vegas, Nevada is the most powerful in the world. The equivalent of 40 billion candle power, the beam is visible to aeroplanes from a distance of 250 miles.

Superman first appeared lifting a car on the cover of "Action Comic" in June 1938. If you have a copy of that particular issue, you could sell it now and buy a house with the money. Originally, he couldn't fly, only leap up to two hundred metres or so, but his super powers have got stronger and stronger as time has gone on.

**The fattest ever international footballer was Willie Henry Foulke, an England goalkeeper who weighed in at a wobbly 26 stone. His nickname, for some reason, was "Fatty".**

There have been over 20 million Volkswagen Beetles made.

**The first number plates were introduced in Paris in 1893.**

Winston Churchill was a stutterer. As a child, one of his teachers warned, "Because of his stuttering he should be discouraged from following in his father's political footsteps."

**On 5th October 1974, four years, three months and sixteen days after Dave Kunste set out from Minnesota, he became the first man to walk around the world, having taken more than 20 million steps.**

The American Government's nickname, "Uncle Sam", came from Uncle Sam Wilson, a meat inspector in Troy, New York.

**After the French Revolution of 1789, selling sour wine was considered against the national interest and any merchant found doing so was promptly executed.**

The term "It's all fun and games until someone loses an eye" first came from Ancient Rome. The only rule during wrestling matches was "No eye gouging." Everything else was allowed, but the only way to be disqualified was to poke someone's eye out.

The word malaria means "bad air". This derives from the old days when it was thought that all diseases are caused by bad, or dirty air.

The pin that holds a hinge together is called a "pintle".

Contrary to popular belief, elephants are not afraid of mice.

Vincent Van Gogh cut off his right ear. However, his famous painting "Self-portrait with Bandaged Ear" shows the left one bandaged because he painted it using a mirror.

Sherlock Holmes, a resident of London's Baker Street, is the world's most portrayed character. Created by Sir Arthur Conan Doyle, he has made appearances in 211 films.

If you took all the urine the world produces in one day, it would take a full 20 minutes to flow over Niagara Falls!

The area of the earth is almost 200 million square miles.

Earth travels through space at 66,700 miles per hour.

A "funambulist" is a tight-rope walker.

The word "electric" was first used in 1600 by William Gilbert, a doctor to Queen Elizabeth I.

The thin line of cloud that forms behind an aircraft at high altitudes is called a contrail.

An American ton is equivalent to 900 kg (2,000 pounds). A British ton is 1008 kg (2,240 pounds), called a gross ton.

In air, sound travels about 340 metres per second. It travels faster on a hot day.

Ice cream was invented in China in about 200 B.C., when a soft, milk and rice mixture was further thickened by mixing in snow.

Roman noblemen would send their slaves to mountain tops to gather fresh snow. This snow was then flavoured and served as part of their famous food orgies as another early version of ice cream.

Chop suey is a very famous Chinese dish, but it was invented by chefs in an American restaurant. Sweet and sour sauce, another favourite in Chinese take-aways, doesn't exist in China. It was created by Chinese chefs living in the UK for the sweet-toothed British, after noticing their liking for tomato ketchup.

For its size, your tongue is the strongest muscle in your body.

**The Academy Award statue (or "Oscar"), is named after a librarian's uncle. One day Margaret Herrick, librarian for the Academy of Motion Picture Arts and Sciences, made a remark that the statue looked like her uncle Oscar, and the name stuck.**

The country of Sweden has the most phones per person on Earth.

**Honey does not spoil. Honey found in the tombs of Egyptian pharaohs has been tasted by archaeologists and found to be edible.**

Lettuce is a member of the sunflower family.

**Reindeer eat a moss which contains a special chemical that acts as an antifreeze and keeps their body fluids warm.**

The Bible is the world's bestselling book. It is also the one most often stolen from bookshops.

Duke is the highest rank you can be without being a king or a prince.

The longest stairway in the world is the service stairway for the Niesenbahn funicular railway near Spiez, Switzerland. It has 11,674 steps.

The yo-yo is the second oldest known toy in the world (the doll is older); it was invented over 3,000 years ago in Greece.

**There is an airport in Calcutta named "Dum Dum Airport."**

The main library at Indiana University sinks over an inch every year because when it was built, the engineers failed to take into account the weight of all the books that would occupy the building.

**According to ancient law in York, it is perfectly legal to shoot a Scotsman with a bow and arrow, except on Sundays.**

The names of all the continents end with the same letter they start with.

**The "Flower of Kent" is a large green-skinned apple variety, and is thought to have been the kind that hit Sir Isaac Newton on the head, prompting him to explore the theory of gravity.**

The French eat 40,000 metric tons of snails each year. Snails have been eaten as food since at least ancient Roman times. In the oldest surviving cookbook, the author, Apicius, included a recipe for snails.

**The celebration of Christmas was banned in Boston from 1659 to 1681. Anyone showing Christmas spirit was fined five shillings. The pilgrims believed that it was a decadent and ungodly celebration.**

# Did you know…

…that the famous Italian opera singer Luciano Pavarotti was once applauded for an hour and seventeen minutes?

The most populated city in the world - when major urban areas are included - is Tokyo, with 30 million residents.

**The Vatican is the world's smallest country, at 0.44 square kilometres (0.16 square miles).**

Earth is the densest planet in the solar system.

**Fingernails grow nearly four times faster than toenails.**

Alaska has more bears than all the other states in America put together.

**The name Wendy was first used in J.M. Barrie's book "Peter Pan".**

Playing cards in India are round.

**Pioneer aviator Orville Wright wrote numbers on all the eggs that his chickens produced so he could eat them in the order they were laid.**

In 1973, Swedish confectionery salesman Roland Ohlsson was buried in a coffin made entirely of chocolate.

**Mercedes Benz cars are named after a girl called Mercedes Jellinek.**

Coca Cola and Dr. Pepper were both introduced in the same year: 1886.

**One of Queen Victoria's stranger wedding presents was an enormous wheel of Cheddar cheese. It weighed over 1,000 pounds.**

Los Angeles' full name is "El Pueblo de Nuestra Senora la Reina de los Angeles de Porciuncula".

**Right-handed people live, on average, nine years longer than left-handed people do.**

Rubber bands last longer when refrigerated.

**There are 336 dimples on a regulation golf ball.**

There are 701 types of pure breed dogs.

**People who become hysterical when peanut butter sticks to the roof of their mouth are suffering from the condition "arachibutyrophobia".**

In 1921, the commissioner of Ellis Island in New York made the decision to treat all incoming immigrants to a taste of something truly American, by serving them ice cream as part of their first meal.

**The invention of the doughnut is usually attributed to Dutch settlers in Pennsylvania who punched holes in their original Dutch "olykoeks" (oily cakes). The hole in the middle has also been attributed to a New England sea captain, Hanson Gregory, who, in 1847 punched holes in the dough because his mother's doughnuts were never cooked properly in the middle. Neither of them was the first to have this idea though. Archaeologists have found petrified fried cakes with holes in them in the southwestern United States in prehistoric Native American ruins.**

It's easy to remember the order of the planets in our solar system with this line: My Very Eager Mother Just Served Us Nine Pizzas. The capital letters stand for the order of the planets, starting closest to the Sun: Mercury, Venus, Earth, Mars, Jupiter, Saturn, Uranus, Neptune, and Pluto. That is, except for between January 1979 and March 1999 when, because of a large orbital eccentricity, Pluto was closer to the Sun than Neptune.

**Queen Isabella of Castille, who sent Christopher Columbus to find the Americas, boasted that she had only two baths in her life: once at her birth and once before she got married.**

The scientific term for the common tomato is lycopersicon lycopersicum, which means "wolf peach."

**In 1895, French brothers Auguste and Louis Lumière demonstrated a projector system in Paris, and in 1907 they screened the first public movie.**

The electric chair was invented by a dentist.

**Julius Caesar was the first to use coded communications, using what has become known as the Caesar Cipher.**

It takes about 550 peanuts to make a 12-ounce jar of creamy peanut butter.

**Heinz sells more than half of all of the tomato ketchup sold in America.**

Half of the world's supply of raisins are grown in California.

A Californian discovered the commercial potential of raisins quite by accident. In 1873, a freak hot spell withered the grapes on the vine. One enterprising San Francisco grocer advertised these shrivelled grapes as "Peruvian Delicacies" and the rest is history.

The honeybee kills more people world-wide than all the poisonous snakes put together.

**New Year's Day** used to be on **25th of March. It was changed to January 1st in 1600 in Scotland, and in 1751 in England.**

First made at the beginning of the 20th century, lollipops were named after a racehorse of the time, Lolly Pop.

**A hippopotamus can run faster than a man.**

**The liver is the largest of the body's internal organs.**

On average, an attack of the hiccups lasts for five minutes.

**Excavations from Egyptian tombs dating to 5,000 BC show that the ancient Egyptian kids played with toy hedgehogs.**

About 42,000 tennis balls are used the Wimbledon Championship.

**The cruise liner, Queen Elizabeth II, moves about six inches for each gallon of petrol that it burns.**

Wilma Flintstone's maiden name was Wilma Slaghoopal, and Betty Rubble's maiden name was Betty Jean McBricker.

**111,111,111 x 111,111,111 = 12,345,678,987,654,321**

In 1990, The Mars chocolate company decided to change the Marathon bar's name to "Snickers". But Mars didn't want to lose the bar's British fans. So for 18 months, the bar's wrapper wore both the Snickers and Marathon names.

Then the Marathon name was dropped, and Snickers/Marathon went from the UK's 9th best-selling chocolate bar to No. 3. (Kit Kat is No. 1.)

**The melting point of cocoa butter is just below the human body temperature - which is why chocolate literally melts in your mouth.**

John Rolfe married Pocahontas, the Native American princess, in 1613.

# Did you know...

...that microwave ovens were invented by chance in a laboratory accident?

After King Tutankhamen's tomb was discovered in Egypt in 1922, a number of people associated with the discovery died mysterious deaths.

**Was it coincidence... or was it a curse?**

Tutankhamen's tomb was unearthed in November 1922 by Howard Carter, an amateur archeologist commissioned by the English nobleman Lord Carnarvon to find it.

**The discovery of the site was hailed as "the greatest find in the annals of archeology." But soon after the discovery was announced, rumours about a curse on the tomb began to spread. They weren't taken seriously—until Lord Carnarvon came down with a mysterious fever contracted from an insect bite, and died. Even more strange, when the mummy of Tutankhamun was unwrapped in 1925, it was found to have a wound on the left cheek in the exact same position as the insect bite on Carnarvon that lead to his demise.**

The curse rumours strengthened when word came from Lord Carnarvon's home in England at 1:50 a.m.—the exact moment of Lord Carnarvon's death—that his favourite dog had suddenly collapsed, and died.

**By 1929 eleven people connected with the discovery of the Tomb had died of unnatural causes. This included two of Carnarvon's relatives, Carter's personal secretary, Richard Bethell, and Bethell's father, Lord Westbury. Westbury killed himself by jumping from a building.
He left a note that read,
"I really cannot stand any more horrors, so I am making my exit."**

Scottish inventor John Logie Baird gave the first public demonstration of television in 1926 in Soho, London. Ten years later there were only 100 TV sets in the world. Today, there are almost a billion. The first daily TV broadcast was started by the BBC in November 1936.

Mel Blanc, who played the voice of Bugs Bunny, was allergic to carrots.

**A quarter of Russia is covered by forest.**

Although modern images of India often show poverty and lack of development, India was the richest country on earth until the time of British invasion in the early 17th Century.

**Approximately one third of the Earth's land surface is desert.**

Bird droppings are the main export of Nauru, an island in the Western Pacific.

**Cuba is the only island in the Caribbean to have a railway.**

The first documented lighthouse was at Alexandria, built in 200 BC on the island of Pharos by the Egyptian Emperor, Ptolemy. Considered as one of the Seven Wonders of the World, it is thought to have been 150 metres (492 feet) high - about three times taller than modern lighthouses.

**Roman Emperors built many lighthouses to assist their navigators. In 90 AD, the Emperor Caligula ordered a lighthouse at Dover, England. It is the oldest lighthouse in the country and still stands in the grounds of Dover Castle.**

**It's so hot in the Sahara Desert that rain evaporates before it reaches the ground.**

King Charles II first tried dog racing in 1670 at Hampton Court Palace. It wasn't until 250 years later that racing greyhounds took off as a popular sport, largely due to the invention of the mechanical hare. Early hares were mounted on roller skates and pulled along with string.

**Li is the family name for more than 87 million people in China.**

Mongolia is the world's largest landlocked country.

**More than 75% of all the countries in the world are north of the equator.**

Oak trees do not have acorns until they reach 50 years of age.

**The average iceberg weighs 20 million tons.**

The English Channel gets a foot wider every year.

**The Eisenhower interstate road system in America requires that one mile in every five must be straight. These straight parts are for use as airstrips in times of war or other emergencies.**

The fastest moon in our solar system circles Jupiter once every seven hours - travelling at 70,400 miles per hour.

**The nearest neighbour galaxy to our own Milky Way is called "Andromeda".**

The oldest pantomime stories are Aladdin and Cinderella. Both tales date back well over a thousand years. Aladdin originated from ancient Syria, and Cinderella from China. Cinderella's slippers were originally made of fur - they became glass ones due to a dodgy translation some time in history.

A piece of meteorite from Mars about the size of a pea once sold for £4,583. That is over a thousand times its weight in gold.

A cow can give about 200,000 glasses of milk in her lifetime.

The Egyptians were extremely fond of cats. The penalty for an Egyptian killing a cat, 4,000 years ago, was death.

Planet Earth actually rotated faster a hundred million years ago, making each year longer by roughly five days. If you go back further, 600 million years ago, a year lasted 425 days.

WHAT'S THE DATE TODAY?

THE EIGHTY SEVENTH OF DECEMBER

**Diners are part of a rich tradition in America. Over the years, the waitresses and cooks in these local restaurants have even invented their own language for the dishes they prepare.**

"Adam and Eve on a raft" means two poached eggs on toast.

**"Zeppelins in a fog" is sausages and mashed potatoes.**

"Cowboy with spurs" is a western omelette with chips.

**"Stretch" is a Coke.**

"Full house" is a grilled cheese, bacon, and tomato sandwich.

**"Cremate a blue, bikini cut" is a well done, toasted blueberry muffin cut in four pieces.**

"Radio" is a tuna fish sandwich on toast. (Formerly "tuna down" which sounded like "turn it down," as if asking someone to turn down the volume on a radio).

**"51" is hot chocolate.**

"Bucket of cold mud" is a bowl of chocolate ice cream.

**"Squeeze it" means "make it fast".**

"Seaboard" means "make it to take out".

**"Cluck and grunt" is eggs and bacon.**

"Nervous pudding" is jelly.

A dolphin's hearing is so acute that it can pick up an underwater sound from 15 miles away.

**In 1956, there was an iceberg in the South Pacific larger than Belgium.**

In Bangladesh, kids as young as 15 can be jailed for cheating in exams.

**In the Caribbean, there are oysters that can climb trees.**

The oldest exposed surface on Earth is New Zealand's South Island.

**The South Pole is colder than the North Pole.**

You may not think of the flu as a big killer, but in 1918–19 an outbreak of an unusually nasty flu virus killed 25 million people. Causing 18,000 deaths in London alone, it killed more people than the First World War itself.

**M & M's were developed so that soldiers could eat chocolate without getting their fingers sticky.**

Elton John's real name is Reginald Dwight.

**In the remote island on St Kilda, Scotland, letters were once placed in hollowed-out driftwood attached to an inflated sheep's bladder. These were set adrift in the north Atlantic, where current, wind and luck carried mail to shore on the mainland.**

Cranberries are sorted for ripeness by bouncing them; a fully ripened cranberry can be dribbled like a basketball.

The Earth, in its history, has been hit by at least one million meteors.

**About 3,000 stars are visible to the naked eye.**

The left lung is smaller than the right lung to make room for the heart.

**In 1962, the Mashed Potato, the Loco-Motion, the Frug, the Monkey, and the Funky Chicken were popular dances.**

The first live televised murder was in 1963, when Jack Ruby killed President Kennedy's assassin, Lee Harvey Oswald, while millions of viewers watched.

**There are 1,792 steps to the top of the Eiffel Tower.**

A 'jiffy' is an actual unit of time meaning one hundredth of a second.

**Mail has been carried by foot runners, bullock carts, camels and horses. Reindeers have been used in Scandinavia and Russia, dogs in Alaska and cats in Belgium. In 1879, the town of Liege, Belgium employed 37 cats to carry bundles of letters to villages.**

The first 3-D stamp was issued by Italy in 1956. Viewed through special glasses with red and green lenses, the image of the world map appears in 3-D.

**Centuries ago, you could lose your nose, not your freedom, if you broke the law in India. As noses were chopped off so often, there was a big demand for surgeons who could rebuild them.**

# Did you know…

…that the Auditorium organ in Atlantic City, America, is as loud as 25 full brass bands?

**Every major league baseball team in the U.S. buys about 18,000 baseballs each season.**

Every year, Americans dispose of 1.6 billion pens.

**Icelanders read more books per head than any other people in the world.**

If you had money to spend on doctors in Ancient Babylon, you knew you'd be looked after well. After all, the hands were cut off any doctors who killed their patients. In Babylon, doctors didn't come cheap – it cost five gold coins to see one. If you couldn't afford to visit the doctor, you could always take a trip to the market place. Sick people would go there and invite passers-by to give them free medical advice.

**In every episode of "Seinfeld" on TV there is a Superman somewhere.**

In the 18th century, many women went to the trouble of having their gums pierced so they could have hooks fitted to hold their false teeth.

**If a human hair were as thick as a nylon rope, it could support a train engine.**

The "talkies" (films with sound) didn't appear until 1927 – but films before then were far from silent. When you went to see an early film, a presenter called the "master of ceremonies" would read out any words and fill in details of the plot. Specially employed actors would hide behind the screen and speak the actors' lines. Machines, like the "Noiseograph" and "Dramagraph", would add sound effects to the action.

**Easter is the first Sunday after the first full Moon after March 21st.**

The linen bandages that were used to wrap Egyptian mummies averaged 1,000 yards in length.

**Albert Einstein's last words will never be known. He spoke them in German, and his nurse didn't speak any German.**

Jamaica has more churches per square mile than any other country in the world.

"SOS from MGJ – We have struck an iceberg sinking fast come to our assistance." One of the most famous Morse code messages of all time, this desperate plea for help was sent by radio on 14 April 1912 by the radio operator of the Titanic. As the Titanic sank into the icy waters of the Arctic Ocean, the radio operator sent the SOS signal to attract other ships. The first ever message to use the SOS signal, it fired the world's imagination about the new invention called "radio telegraph" – Morse code sent by radio.

According to the ceremonial customs of Orthodox Judaism, it is officially night when you cannot tell the difference between a black thread and a red one.

**The post has been a target for thieves from the day the postal service started. Important mail had a picture of gallows printed on it to warn thieves who couldn't read what would happen if the post was stolen. Stealing Her Majesty's mail carried the death sentence.**

Jeremy Bentham, a British philosopher who died in 1832, left his entire estate to the London Hospital provided that his body be allowed to preside over its board meetings. His skeleton was clothed and fitted with a wax mask of his face. It was present at the meeting for 92 years.

**Strawberries have more vitamin C in them than oranges.**

The female spider is generally bigger and stronger than the male, and after mating, she will often eat her boyfriend as a snack. Male spiders wanting to avoid this experience generally approach females with a nice juicy fly neatly wrapped up in silk as a present.

**Ketchup is excellent for cleaning brass with.**

The first police force was established in Paris, in 1667.

**The shortest war in history was between Zanzibar and England in 1896. Zanzibar surrendered after 38 minutes.**

In 1992, Frank Perkins of Los Angeles made an attempt on the world record for sitting on top of a flagpole. Suffering from the flu he came down eight hours short of the 400-day record to find that his sponsor had gone bust, his girlfriend had left him and his phone and electricity had been cut off.

**The first airmail service carried letters only 20 kilometres. Taking off on 9th September 1911, it flew mail from one side of London to the other.**

**It takes 4,000 crocus flowers to produce a single ounce of the spice called saffron.**

One in five of the world's doctors is Russian.

**The son of a Malagasy Indian has no right to be taller than his father. If he does get above himself, he must buy the right with money or an ox.**

There are ten human body parts that are only three letters long: eye, hip, arm, leg, ear, toe, jaw, rib, lip and gum.

**Wolfgang Amadeus Mozart was born in Salzburg in Austria. By eight years old, he had written his first symphony, and could play any piece on the piano. He often played blindfolded to impress.**

Nearly 50% of all bank robberies take place on Friday, largely because shops go to the bank with the week's takings on a Friday afternoon.

FRI
24
JUNE

"Alan Smithee" is a name that filmmakers use when they don't want their real names to appear in the credits because the movie turned out to be terrible.

The oldest document in Latin is in a woman's handwriting - it dates from the first century A.D. - and is an invitation to a birthday party.

The oldest letter in Britain is also an invitation to a birthday party. Sent by a Roman to his friend at Hadrian's Wall, the letter is about 1,900 years old.

The Roman postal service was so good, it could carry a letter from London to Cardiff in only three days.

1961 was the most recent year that could be written upside-down and right side-up and appear the same. The next year that this will be possible will be 6009.

The best greyhound ever was called Mick the Miller. In three years racing on English soil, he didn't lose a single race.

Raw cashews are poisonous.

Victorian villains William Burke and William Hare used to dig up the dead and sell them to medical students. They stole bodies from graves in Edinburgh and sold them on to a doctor named Robert Knox. Word about these fiendish men soon spread. After loved-ones died in Edinburgh, terrified relatives would cover their graves with heavy iron grilles to keep the evil pair at bay. Deciding to look elsewhere for corpses, Burke and Hare turned to murder to keep up with the growing demand for the dead.

The magic word "Abracadabra" was originally intended for the specific purpose of curing hay fever.

**The best place in the world to see a rainbow is Honolulu in Hawaii. In the morning, or at sunset, the sky becomes orange and the rainbows, instead of being multicoloured, are bright red.**

The abbreviation e.g. stands for "Exempli gratia", or "For example."

**Of all the big cats, only three of them—lions, tigers and leopards—can roar.**

In Nairobi, Kenya, leopards steal food from people's dustbins.

**The £20 note is the most commonly forged in Britain. The one featuring a portrait of Edward Elgar had a number of new details built into it, including the latest anti-counterfeiting technology. The Bank of England said it had several reasons for chosing Elgar for the note, one of which was that the Victorian composer had a very fine, large and bushy moustache, which would be very difficult to copy.**

The average cost of rehabilitating a seal after the Exxon Valdez oil spill in Alaska was 80,000 dollars. At a special ceremony, two of these expensively saved animals were released back into the wild amid cheers and applause from onlookers. Unfortunately a minute later they were both eaten by a Killer Whale.

**French President Charles de Gaulle's final words were: "It hurts."**

**There are more than 23,000 black taxi cabs working in London.**

The Death's-head Moth, Britain's largest moth, has an unusual fondness for honey. It has developed a little squeak that it uses to let bees know it is about to enter their hive. The password seems to work, because the bees let the moth come in and stuff its face without getting annoyed.

**Air becomes liquid at about minus 190 degrees Celsius. Liquid air looks like water with a bluish tint.**

In 1949, forecasting the relentless march of science, "Popular Mechanics" magazine said "Computers in the future may weigh no more than one and a half tons."

**The only 15-letter word that can be spelled without repeating a letter is "uncopyrightable".**

The word "facetious" contains all the vowels in the correct order.

**The furthest long-distance phone call ever was between two people over a third of a million kilometres apart. The historic chat, on 24 July 1969, took place between US President Richard Nixon and American astronauts Neil Armstrong and Buzz Aldrin. Nixon, phoning from the White House, spoke to Armstrong and Aldrin while they were on the Moon.**

In the 1930s, special blue post boxes appeared in Britain that were specially for air mail. Although these used to be a regular sight on the streets, they have since disappeared.

# Did you know...

...that a fully-grown python can swallow a pig whole?

**The first paper was made when dinosaurs still roamed the Earth. Using dried wood mashed into a pulp, the earliest papermakers were wasps. These insects, who have always built their own nests from home-made paper, learnt the art of papermaking 300 million years before humans did.**

Our eyes are always the same size from birth, but our nose and ears never stop growing.

**The longest word in the English language, according to the Oxford English Dictionary, is "pneumonoultramicro-scopicsilicovolcanoconiosis."**

Canada is an Indian word meaning "Big Village."

**The Amazon rainforest produces half the world's oxygen supply.**

In the 1580s, a chain of warning bonfires across Britain could send only two messages. One was "Help! The Spanish invaders are coming!" and the other was "Oh no! The Spanish invaders are here!" Compare that to the clever system the Ancient Greeks put together over 2,400 years ago. Using sets of five torches, it could send any letter of the Greek alphabet. The people who ran it burned different combinations of torches to send different letters. Although it must have been quite slow, the Ancient Greeks were able to use this system on every hilltop to send detailed messages from town to town.

**Venetian blinds did not originate in Venice: they were invented in Japan.**

The average human eats about eight spiders in their lifetime while asleep.

**The Three-Toed Sloth is the slowest animal in the world. It can take it three days to climb a medium-sized tree.**

Emus lay emerald green eggs.

**The huge clock on the British Houses of Parliament was once slowed down when a passing group of starlings decided to take a breather on the minute hand.**

99% of the matter in our solar system is contained in the Sun.

**Dissolved salt makes up 3.5 per cent of the ocean.**

Despite a population of over a billion, China has only about 200 family names.

**The Geysir ('gusher') near Mount Hekla in south-central Iceland, after which all other geysers are named, shoots hot water up to 180 feet in the air.**

The Post Office published a leaflet in 1782 telling people to chop banknotes in half before they sent them in the post. If the two halves of a banknote were posted at different times, a highwayman wouldn't be able to steal it.

**Dinosaur droppings are called coprolites.**

Many loving parents of the 1760s plunged their children into ice-cold water every morning. They thought a freezing dip would help their little darlings ward off colds and other diseases.

The mistakenly named East Alligator River in Australia's Northern Territory doesn't contain any alligators - they are crocodiles.

**Swiss cars have the letters CH on their identity stickers, and the Swiss have the e-mail address CH. This is because the official name of Switzerland is "Confederation Helvetica."**

Hawaii is home to the world's largest active volcano, Mauna Loa, which is 120 km long and 4,170 metres high. Most of Mauna Loa is underwater. The last time it erupted was in 1984.

**An elephant trunk has no bone but 40,000 muscles.**

Cockney rhyming slang comes from the East End of London. Originally from market traders, it was used to confuse outsiders when the traders talked among themselves. Rhyming phrases are used to replace common words, and the rhyming part is then dropped. For example:

**"Got to me mickey, found me way up the apples, put on me whistle when the dog went. It was me trouble telling me to fetch the saucepans."**

Translation:

"Got to my house (mickey mouse), found my way up the stairs (apples and pears), put on my suit (whistle and flute) when the phone (dog and bone) rang. It was my wife (trouble and strife) telling me to fetch the kids (saucepan lids)."

**The average raindrop falls at seven miles per hour.**

**You burn more calories sleeping than you do watching television.**

The national anthem of Greece has 158 verses.

**Nepal is the only country that has a non-rectangular flag.**

Until 1965, driving in Sweden was done on the left-hand side of the road. The changeover was done on a weekday at 5:00 p.m. This was supposed to prevent people from waking up in the morning and forgetting which side of the road to drive on.

**Kittens begin dreaming at just over one week old.**

Insurance companies require car drivers making claims to fill out forms explaining very briefly the cause of their accidents. These forms often reveal interesting versions of the events. Here are some genuine extracts from actual forms:

"I thought my window was down, but I found out it was up when I put my head through it."

**"A truck backed through my windscreen into my wife's face."**

"I pulled away from the side road, looked at my mother-in-law, and drove over the embankment."

**"In an attempt to kill a fly, I drove into the telephone pole."**

"I had been driving for 40 years when I fell asleep at the wheel and had an accident."

**"To avoid hitting the bumper of the car in front, I struck the pedestrian."**

"The pedestrian had no idea which direction to turn, so I ran over him."

**"The indirect cause of the accident was a little guy in a small car with a big mouth."**

"I was thrown from my car as it left the road. I was later found in a ditch by some stray dogs."

**"The guy was all over the road, I had to swerve my car several times before I finally hit him."**

**Turtles can live for more than 100 years.**

The Cicada, an insect found in Africa, spends 17 years of its life sleeping. It wakes up for just two weeks during which it mates and then dies.

**You're just as likely to die by falling out of bed then you are to get struck by lightning; each is a 1 in 2,000,000 chance. You have a 1 in 3,000,000 chance of being killed by a snake, and the odds against a person being struck by a meteorite are about 10 trillion to one.**

The Sun's warming rays travel through 93 million miles of space to reach Earth. Moving at the speed of light, they make the trip in just eight minutes. A jet airliner would need more than 18 years to complete the same journey.

**Jupiter's moon, Io, has the most spectacular scenery in the solar system. Io's low gravity means that its volcanoes can throw boiling rock 50 miles into the air.**

The United States produces 19 per cent of the world's rubbish.

**The tallest sand dunes found anywhere in the world are in the Sahara Desert. A single dune has enough sand in it to bury the Eiffel Tower.**

In the first scene of Disney's "The Little Mermaid", the camera pans across the crowd awaiting the entrance of King Neptune. Look closely and in the crowd you can see Goofy, Mickey Mouse and Donald Duck eating popcorn.

There are a thousand times more living things in the sea than there are on land.

**A typical lightning bolt is three inches wide and two miles long.**

During the French "Reign of Terror", from 1793 to 1794, 500,000 people were arrested and 17,000 of them had their heads chopped off.

**The British flag is not "The Union Jack" – it's actually "The Union Flag". It is called the Union Jack only when out at sea on navy ships.**

In the 1790s, loud horns and electric shocks were used to make sure the dead were really dead. At that time, there were lots of horror stories around about people being accidentally buried alive. Very few of them were actually true but that didn't stop people from ordering bells and other devices to be put on their graves. These would enable them to sound the alarm if there had been a terrible mistake. A common way to check if someone was dead was to put a mirror in front of their mouth. The slightest breath would make the mirror go cloudy, telling you the person was still alive.

**For some reason "Harry Potter and the Philosopher's Stone" is called "Harry Potter and the Sorcerer's Stone" in America. Every time the name of the stone is mentioned in the film it had to be filmed once as "sorcerer's stone" and then again as "philosopher's stone".**

The bagpipe was originally made from the whole skin of a dead sheep.

...that for her Silver Wedding Anniversary, the country of Cameroon gave Queen Elizabeth II an elephant?

**The Poison-Arrow Frog has enough poison in its body to kill about 2,200 people.**

Earth is slowing down - in a few million years' time we won't need to have a leap year because one orbit of the planet will take exactly 365 days.

**One-quarter of the brain is used to control the eyes.**

Kiwi birds are blind - they hunt by smell.

**The Mola Mola, or Ocean Sunfish, lays up to five million eggs at one time.**

84,119,500 pound coins were made by the Royal Mint in the year 2000 alone.

**Different designs are available representing English, Scottish, Welsh and Irish pound coins. Around the edge of each coin is a phrase, some of which are:**

**NEMO ME IMPUNE LACESSIT**
"No one provokes me with impunity"
(Latin)

**PLEIDIOL WYF I'M GWLAD**
"True am I to my country"
(Welsh, from the Welsh National Anthem)

**DECUS ET TUTAMEN**
"An ornament and a safeguard"
(Latin)

**In the film "Harry Potter and the Philosopher's Stone", a young actor named Joe Sowerbutts provided the voice of Harry Potter when the voice of the original actor, Daniel Radcliffe, started to break.**

Over the last 150 years the average height of people in industrialised nations increased by 10 cm (4 in).

## On average, you speak about 5,000 words every day.

In 1810, German inventor Samuel Soemmering invented the bubble telegraph to send long-distance messages. His invention used electricity passed through wires to make pockets of gas bubble up in a tank of acid. Soemmering had 26 different wires sitting in the acid, one for each letter of the alphabet. If he sent a small current of electricity down any of the wires, a stream of bubbles would appear in the acid at the other end, enabling him to send messages, one letter at a time.

## Sound travels through water three times faster than through air.

The Honey Badger can withstand hundreds of African Bee stings that would kill any other animal.

## During most of the Earth's history, the North and South Poles have been completely free of ice.

In the late 19th century, millions of human mummies were used as fuel for locomotive trains in Egypt where wood and coal was scarce, but mummies were plentiful.

**The expression "long in the tooth", meaning "old", was originally used to describe horses. As horses age, their gums recede, giving the impression that their teeth are growing. The longer the teeth look, the older the horse.**

**The winter of 1932 was so cold that Niagara Falls froze solid.**

The American volcano Mount St Helens was 1,313 feet shorter after erupting in 1980.

**Mountains are formed by a process called orogeny.**

85,000,000 tons of paper are used each year in America.

**Alaska has 29 volcanoes.**

The average life-span of a major league baseball is seven pitches.

**According to the very old poem "T'was the Night Before Christmas", the names of Santa's eight reindeer were: Dasher, Dancer, Prancer, Vixen, Comet, Cupid, Donner and Blitzen.**

The biggest palace on Earth is the Imperial Palace in Beijing. It is so huge you could sleep in a different room every night for 25 years.

**The Great Wall of China is 3,460 kilometres long. It was built over a period of 2,000 years and has 25,000 watchtowers along its length. It isn't a problem getting people to man the towers though, because the Chinese army has about three million soldiers in it.**

Nine is considered the luckiest number worldwide.

**Between 1931 and 1969 Walt Disney collected 35 Oscars.**

# The world's longest game of Monopoly lasted more than 660 hours.

The average human brain has about 100 billion nerve cells.

Nerve impulses to and from the brain travel at 170 miles per hour.

## Most cars honk in the key of F.

At the age of 26, Michelangelo began sculpting his monumental statue of David. He finished it 17 months later, in January, 1504.

A hollowed-out pumpkin with a candle inside - a Jack-O-Lantern - is placed in a window or doorway at Hallowe'en in order to scare off witches and to guard against evil spirits. Ancient Celtic people are thought to have started this tradition in the olden days, only they used real heads, chopped off the bodies of their enemies.

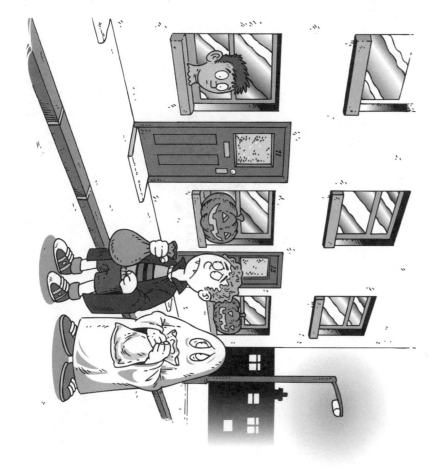

**The following are genuine instructions displayed for English-speaking visitors from businesses around the world.**

Car rental brochure in Tokyo: "When passenger of foot heave in sight, tootle the horn. Trumpet him melodiously at first, but if he still obstacles your passage then tootle him with vigor."

**On a menu of a Polish hotel:**
**"Salad a firm's own make; limpid red beer soup with cheesy dumplings in the form of a finger; roasted duck let loose; beef rashers beaten up in the country people's fashion."**

Japanese instructions on an air conditioner: "Cooles & Heates: If you want just condition of warm in your room, please control yourself."

**In a Hong Kong dress shop:**
**"Order your summers suit. Because is big rush we will execute customers in strict rotation."**

In an East African newspaper: "A new swimming pool is rapidly taking shape since the contractors have thrown in the bulk of their workers."

**In a Vienna hotel:**
**"In case of fire, do your utmost to alarm the porter."**

Copenhagen airline ticket office: "We take your bags and send them in all directions."

On the lion cage at a zoo in the Czech Republic: "No smoothen the lion."

# Did you know...

...that in Florida, it is illegal for women to parachute on Sundays, unless they are married?

The wind carries about 100 million tons of sand around the Earth every year.

**Light can travel around the Earth at its equator seven and a half times in one second.**

Earth's oceans are an average of two miles deep.

**On his way home to visit his parents, a college student fell between two trains at the station in Jersey City, New Jersey, and was rescued by an actor on his way to visit a sister in Philadelphia. The student was Robert Lincoln, heading for Washington. The actor was Edwin Booth, the brother of the man who, a few weeks later, would murder the student's father, President Abraham Lincoln.**

Before ancient surgeons made their first incision, they sometimes covered their patients with wet clay. They realised that sick people were often hot around the part of them that was causing trouble, as bodies heat up when they fight off diseases. When surgeons smeared clay on their patient's bodies, they found it often dried quickest over the poorly body parts. The drying clay gave them a good idea where they should do their work.

**Every time you lick a stamp, you're consuming one tenth of a calorie.**

The longest place name in Britain is in Wales: Llanfairpwllgwyngyllgogerychwyrndrobwllllantysiliogogogoch. It means "St Mary's Church in the hollow of the white hazel near to the rapid whirlpool of Llantysilio of the red cave".

**Pound for pound, hamburgers cost more than new cars.**

It takes 3,000 cows to supply the U.S. National Football League with enough leather for a year's supply of footballs.

**On average, 100 people choke to death on ballpoint pens every year.**

A French schoolboy, Claude Chappe, went to great lengths to send messages to his brother. Using two wooden arms mounted on a long, high pole, he put together a system that could send thousands of different words. Chappe could tilt the two arms at different angles just by turning some handles. Different arm positions stood for different words. As the arms were high up in the air, his brother could see them if he was a few hundred metres away. In the 1770s, Chappe gave his invention to the French revolutionaries. This system, called semaphore, was also adopted by the British who used it to keep in touch about the Battle of Waterloo.

**The world's most valuable Barbie doll is the 40th Anniversary De Beers customized doll. It cost £60,000 and wore a total of 22 carats of diamonds.**

A group of crows is called a "murder".

**Duelling is legal in Paraguay as long as both parties are registered blood donors.**

An ostrich can run up to 70 kph (43 mph).

**The eruption of the Krakatoa volcano was equal in power to the detonation of 223 million tons of dynamite.**

A female kangaroo is called a Flyer, and a male is called a Boomer.

**A lion's roar can be heard from five miles away.**

The male Gypsy Moth can smell the virgin female Gypsy Moth from two miles away.

**Chickens that lay brown eggs have red ear lobes. There is a genetic link between the two.**

A pregnant goldfish is called a twit.

**During World War II, Americans tried to train bats to drop bombs.**

The world's worst earthquake occured in 1556 in China, killing approximately 830,000 people.

**Palindromes are words and sentences that read the same backwards as forwards, like BOB or LEVEL. The following are all palidromes:**

A man, a plan, a canal, Panama!

**Are we not drawn onward, we few, drawn onward to new era?**

A Toyota. Race fast, safe car. A Toyota!

**Doc, note I dissent a fatness. I diet on cod!**

Go hang a salami, I'm a lasagna hog!

**No lemons, no melon!**

Yawn. Madonna fan? No damn way!

**In its entire lifetime, the average worker bee will produce only one teaspoonful of honey.**

The first city to reach a population of one million people was Rome in 133 B.C. London reached the mark in 1810 and New York made it in 1875. Today, there are over 300 cities in the world that boast a population in excess of one million.

**The phrase "rule of thumb" is derived from an old English law which stated that you couldn't beat your wife with anything wider than your thumb.**

Some words you can write upside down with a pocket calculator are:
Hello, Boss, Sheesh, Obesehog, Biggles and Bobsleigh.

**The colder the room you sleep in, the better the chances are that you'll have a bad dream.**

It is a lot harder to learn how to write in Chinese than English, because there are no letters in Chinese, only words. Each word has its own symbol, and over 2,000 of them are used in everyday speech.
It is the oldest written language surviving, dating back probably 7,000 years.

**The most expensive car number plate in the world was bought in Hong Kong in 1994. The plate was "9", which in Cantonese - the language spoken in Hong Kong - sounds like the word for Dog. 1994 was the Chinese Year of the Dog, so it was considered very lucky.**
**The new owner payed 15 million Hong Kong dollars for his new number.**

In 1987, a 1,000cc motorbike travelled one mile at the Illawarra mini bike training club in New South Wales, Australia. It was carrying 46 passengers.

**In Italy, a campaign for Schweppes Tonic Water translated the name into "Schweppes Toilet Water".**

November - when translated literally - means the ninth month, even though these days it is the eleventh month of the year.

**The phrase "Often a bridesmaid, but never a bride" actually comes from an advertisement for Listerine mouthwash.**

Scallops are jet-propelled.
The sea creature compresses the valves of its shell and forces water backward in jets near the shell hinge. The force drives the scallop in the direction of the shell opening.

**Earth's atmosphere is, proportionally, thinner than the skin of an apple.**

There are over 50,000 earthquakes on Earth every year.

**The Canadian city of Toronto's original name was York, but it had another name long ago. It was called "the meeting place" by the Ojibway tribe of Southern Ontario. Their word for this? "Toronto".**

Only one person in two billion will live to be 116 or older.

**A pineapple is a berry.**

Leonardo's painting, Mona Lisa, is the most famous art object on Earth, but it's not insured. It is so valuable, no-one can afford the payments.

**If each count were one second long, it would take about twelve days to count to a million, and 32 years to count to a billion.**

The ingredients in Lea and Perrins Worcestershire sauce are stirred together and allowed to sit for two years before being bottled.

**The words for the American national anthem, "Star Spangled Banner", were written by Francis Scott Key, but the tune was originally from an ancient Greek drinking song called "Anacrean in Heaven".**

The word "girl" appears only once in the Bible.

**It is illegal to say "Oh, Boy" in Jonesboro, Georgia.**

It is against the law to fish from horseback in Utah.

**Idaho state law makes it illegal for a man to give his sweetheart a box of chocolates weighing less than 50 pounds.**

In Denver, it is unlawful to lend your vacuum cleaner to your next door neighbour.

**In Devon, Connecticut, it is unlawful to walk backwards after sunset.**

No one may catch fish with his bare hands in Kansas.

**In Memphis, Tennessee, a law still states that it is illegal for a woman to drive a car unless there is a man either running or walking in front of it waving a red flag to warn approaching motorists and pedestrians.**

A law in West Virginia states that "No children may attend school with their breath smelling of wild onions."

**It is illegal in Minnesota to hang male and female underwear on the same washing line.**

In Normal, Oklahoma you could be sent to prison for "making an ugly face at a dog."

**And if you're in Hawaii and laughing at these odd laws, stop! In Hawaii it is against the law to laugh after 10pm.**

130

# Did you know…

…that non-dairy creamers
are highly flammable?

40% of McDonald's profits come from the sales of Happy Meals.

**A bowling pin has to tilt only 7.5 degrees in order to fall down.**

A cat is more inclined to watch TV than a dog, says the experts.

**A cow in Thailand says "oo-ah".**

A dog can suffer from tonsillitis, but not appendicitis. They don't have an appendix.

**Alexander Graham Bell, inventor of the telephone, also set a world water-speed record of over 70 miles an hour at the age of 72.**

Alexander the Great made his soldiers keep clean-shaven so the enemy couldn't grab them by the beards and stab them with their swords.

**"Almost" is the longest word you can make in the English language with all the letters in the correct alphabetical order.**

In 1870, the city of Paris was under seige. People could get messages out of the city only by flying them out on pigeons. Parisians photographed important messages then shrank the photographs to a fraction of their size using a new process called 'microphotography'. They stuffed tiny microphotographs into a quill which they tied to a pigeon's tail feathers. Only one in 20 pigeons got out of Paris safely but each one carried no less than 3,200 messages.

**In 1976 a South American Guppy became the first fish in space.**

The Sun travels at a speed of 155 miles per second, but it still takes 230 million years for it to complete a single revolution of the galaxy.

## The world's highest city is Lhasa, in Tibet.

Worldwide, about 40 square miles of land are transformed into desert each day.

## An annoyed camel will spit at a person.

Canada has one-third of all the fresh water in the world.

**Damascus, Syria, was flourishing a couple of thousand years before Rome was founded in 753 BC, making it the oldest continuously inhabited city in existence.**

7,000 years ago, the Egyptians bowled on alleys not unlike the ones we use today.

**The length from your wrist to your elbow is the same as the length of your foot.**

Kidneys are organs that clean the blood. Almost everyone has two kidneys but most of us could survive with only one of them. In 1954, a patient of the doctors J. Hartwell Harrison and Joseph Murray was very ill because he had no working kidneys at all. He needed a new kidney urgently – one that was very like his own so his body wouldn't reject it. Luckily for him, he had an identical twin. In the first truly successful transplant of its kind, his twin gave him one of his kidneys, saving his life.

**About one-tenth of the earth's surface is permanently covered with ice.**

**In ancient Rome, nobody was allowed to leave a theatre while Emperor Nero was singing. A favourite escape plan for reluctant listeners was to pretend to be dead and be carried out by doctors.**

Donald Westerholt was jailed for 50 years in Houston, Texas, in January 1983 for shoplifting a pair of shoes worth 20 dollars.

**In the 1350s, doctors treating patients in plague-hospitals used to shout their instructions from the street. At that time there was no cure for this deadly disease so doctors were too frightened to go near their infected patients.**

"Spooky," a blue Russian cat, and "George," a Boston terrier, were the first animals in America to be fitted with prescription contact lenses.

**Tokyo, capital of Japan, is one of the world's biggest and most overcrowded cities. Men known as "pushers" are employed to pack people into the city's crowded trains.**

In 1995, fifteen iguanas were accidentally swept out to sea on a raft of water-logged trees. The reptile sailors travelled over 200 miles from Guadeloupe to Anguilla in the Caribbean, arriving safely.

**A millionaire is someone who owns £1 million. If a millionaire changed all his or her money into £1 coins and piled them up on the top of one another, the pile would be 3,000 metres (9,843 feet) high. That's more than twice as high as Britain's tallest mountain (Ben Nevis) and nearly a third of the height of Mount Everest.**

**Akbar the Great, an Indian leader of the 16th Century, kept over a thousand cheetahs for hunting gazelle and hares.**

In the 1938 World Cup Semi-Final in France, the Italian captain, Meazza, scored the winning goal against Brazil with a penalty. In front of a packed stadium and all the world press, his torn shorts then fell down to his ankles.

## Polar Bears are left-handed.

There are two high tides every day. The highest high tides in the world are in the Bay of Fundy between Nova Scotia and New Brunswick on the east coast of Canada. Here the water level at high tide can be 14.5m (47ft) above that at low tide - that is about as high as a five-storey house.

**The world's tallest mountain, measured from its base on the ocean floor, is Mauna Kea on the island of Hawaii. It is 32,000 feet (9,750 metres) tall, about 3,000 feet taller than Mount Everest.**

**The average density of the universe, including stars, planets, asteroids, meteorites and intergalactic fog, is approximately one atom of matter to every 5.5 litres of space.**

The daily heat output of the average man would boil 30 litres of freezing water.

**A 1,200-pound horse eats about seven times its own weight each year.**

Two hundred years ago, pregnant women in France were told to look at nice things if they wanted pretty babies. They were also expected to dwell on lovely thoughts and to read slushy books with happy endings. They were urged to avoid looking at bears and other zoo animals at all costs. Even though people were aware that children looked like their parents, many of them were convinced that a mother's actions had a big effect on her baby's appearance. In the 1600s, a hospital in Louvain, France was so worried about mothers having ugly babies, it banned ugly doctors.

**Men laugh longer, more loudly, and more often, than women.**

Ocean waves will travel thousands of kilometres, provided there is no land in the way to stop them. Waves which begin in the Indian Ocean can travel 19,000 km (11,807 miles) all the way to Alaska.

**One million seconds is equal to 11 days, 13 hours, 46 minutes and 40 seconds.**

In Turkey in the 16th century, anyone caught drinking coffee was condemned to death by law.

When two dogs approach each other, the more dominant one will wag its tail slowly and the less dominant one will wag more quickly. If both of them wag slowly, there is a good chance that there will be a fight.

China's Beijing Duck Restaurant can seat 9,000 people at one time.

**To make haggis, the national dish of Scotland: take the heart, liver, lungs, and small intestine of a calf or sheep, boil them in the stomach of the animal, season with salt, pepper and onions, add suet and oatmeal.**

Humans shed and regrow outer skin cells about every 27 days - almost 1,000 new skins in a lifetime. By 70 years old, an average person will have shed 105 pounds of skin.

**The feet account for one quarter of all the human body's bones.**

Women's hearts beat faster than men's.

**A "clue" originally meant a ball of thread, which is why you "unravel" a mystery.**

A frightened squid will squirt a kind of ink into the water surrounding it. The ink spreads out in a black cloud and hides the squid so it can make its escape.

**The highest cliffs in the world are in Hawaii. They rise just over 1,000m (3,281ft) from the sea. If you threw a stone off the top, it would take about 15 seconds before you heard the splash.**

A company in Taiwan makes dinnerware out of wheat, so you can eat your plate.

A "walla-walla" scene in a film is one where the people in crowd scenes pretend to be talking in the background. When they all say "walla-walla", it looks like they are talking about something.

Armoured knights used to raise their visors to identify themselves when they rode past their king. This custom has become the modern military salute.

Leonardo da Vinci invented scissors.

It's against the law to have a pet in Iceland.

The snail mates only once in its entire life.

Scorpions can withstand 200 times more nuclear radiation than humans can.

In Japan, watermelons are grown square. It's easier to stack them that way.

US presidents John Adams and Thomas Jefferson both died on July 4, 1826. This was 50 years to the day after they signed the Declaration of Independence.

The vibration of shell-like rings on the end of a rattlesnake's tail makes the rattling sound. The rattle is made up of dry, hard pieces of skin. As the snake grows, the number of rings increases. So the louder the rattle, the bigger the snake.

People who live in the desert do not wash up with water, they use sand to clean their dirty dishes.

# Did you know…

…that the 7-ton Stegosaurus had a 2-ounce brain, making it possibly the stupidest animal ever?

**A lion in the wild usually makes no more than 20 kills a year.**

Sweden has the least number of murders annually.

**Icelanders consume more Coca-Cola per head than any other nation.**

A snail can sleep for three years.

**There are eight peas in the average pod.**

If you were young and short of cash 300 years ago, you could always sell your teeth. As the rich ate lots of sugary foods but rarely bothered to clean their teeth, there was always a ready market for young, healthy gnashers. Some people preferred to buy false teeth made of hippopotamus ivory. Others spent their money on "Waterloo teeth" – teeth that had been extracted from dead soldiers on the battlefield at Waterloo.

**In the year 2000 in Sydney, Australia, 120 men named Henry were involved in a mass brawl during a "My Name is Henry" convention. Henry Pantie of Canberra accused Henry Pap of Sydney of not being a Henry at all, but in fact an Angus. "It was a lie," explained Mr Pap, "I'm a Henry and always will be." Henry Pap attacked Henry Pantie, whilst two other Henrys - Jones and Dyer - attempted to pull them apart. Several more Henrys - Smith, Calderwood and Andrews - became involved and soon the entire convention descended into a giant fist fight. The brawl was eventually broken up by riot police, led by a man named Shane.**

**Isaac Newton was only 23 years old when he came up with his "Universal Laws of Gravity".**

"Tom Sawyer" author, Mark Twain's real name was Samuel Clemens. He worked on a riverboat when he was a teenager, where the shout "Mark twain!" meant that the water had reached the second mark on a stick and was therefore deep enough for the big boat to proceed safely.

**In ancient Rome, it was considered a sign of leadership to be born with a crooked nose.**

Most people have an IQ in the 90-109 range. You're considered a genius if your IQ is 132 or above.

**The highest tide in the world is in the Bay of Fundy, Canada, where there is a rise of 53 feet (16 metres).**

The song with the longest title is "I'm a Cranky Old Yank in a Clanky Old Tank on the Streets of Yokohama with my Honolulu Mama Doin' Those Beat-o, Beat-o Flat-On-My-Seat-o, Hirohito Blues" written by Hoagy Carmichael in 1943.

### Bolivia has two capitals.

In January 2000, Kathleen Robertson of Austin, Texas was awarded $780,000 by a jury after breaking her ankle tripping over a toddler who was running amok inside a furniture shop. The owners of the store were understandably surprised at the verdict, considering the misbehaving child was Ms Robertson's own son.

Birds played a role in aerial warfare during World War 1. Because of their acute hearing, parrots were kept on the Eiffel Tower to warn of approaching aircraft long before the planes were heard or seen by human spotters.

**During the high Middle Ages, there was, on the average, a church for every 200 people.**

In the eleventh century, Benedict IX was Pope at eleven years old.

**If your cat is 3, then it is 21 in human years. If your cat is 8, it is 40 in human years. If your cat is 14, it is 70 in human years.**

The word "assassination" was invented by Shakespeare.

**The world's largest alphabet is the Cambodian one, with 74 letters.**

A single dollar share of Coca-Cola stock, purchased in 1919, when the company went public, would have been worth $92,500 in 1997.

**A shrew can starve to death if it doesn't eat every two hours.**

Legendary human rights campaigner Martin Luther King Jr was originally named Michael, like his father. When Junior was 5, Dad changed both their names to Martin.

**The only married couple to fly together in space were Jan Davis and Mark Lee, who flew aboard the Endeavour space shuttle in 1992.**

A day is the time it takes the Earth to spin round once. A year is the time it takes the Earth to go round the Sun.

**The top 109 highest mountains in the world are all in Asia and 96 of them are in the Himalayas.**

Russian president Nikita Khrushchev credited Spam for keeping the Soviet Army alive during World War II. "We had lost our most fertile, food-bearing lands, the Ukraine and the Northern Caucasians. Without SPAM, we wouldn't have been able to feed our army."

**"The Practioner", a British medical journal, has stated that bird-watching may be dangerous to your health. The magazine has officially designated bird-watching a "hazardous hobby", after the death of a weekend bird-watcher who became so involved in his subject that he didn't pay attention to his surroundings and consequently was eaten by a crocodile.**

The world's fastest truck is owned by Les Shockley of Kansas, USA. It goes 376 miles per hour (605 kph).

**Thomas Edison, with 1,093 patents, was the most inventive person ever.**

The first record ever made was "Mary Had a Little Lamb" by inventor Thomas Edison. You couldn't really dance to it, but everyone was really impressed at the time...

**The biggest island in the world is Greenland, with a massive 2.17 million square kilometres. The biggest island in Europe is Great Britain. It is ten times smaller than Greenland, with just 216,777 square kilometres of land.**

Count Dracula has appeared in movies more often than any other horror character. The world's top vampire has clocked up 161 appearances.

**In the middle of the Mojave Desert in California, sits a telephone booth, 50 miles from Interstate 15, in the middle of nowhere. It was built years ago for miners who worked nearby. Today you can get to it on rough tracks. It has a cult following now, with people from all over the world calling and visiting it.**

A mechanical engineer named Elijah McCoy invented a device in the 1870s to oil train wheels while the train kept running. It was called a "lubricator". He made several others for various machines. Though other imitation lubricators followed, none worked as well as the original.
The phrase was coined, "The Real McCoy" to specify Elijah's original versions.

**Americans consume 42 tons of aspirin per day.**

The last execution in the Tower of London took place on Thursday, August 14, 1941. Josef Jakobs, a German spy, was shot by an eight-man firing squad. Because he had suffered a broken ankle when he had parachuted into England on the night of January 31, 1941, he had to be seated in an old Windsor chair.

**Although identified with Scotland, bagpipes are actually a very ancient instrument, introduced into the British Isles by the Romans.**

The length of the finger dictates how fast the fingernail grows, so the nail on your middle finger grows the fastest.

**In September, 1752, the "Julian" calendar was replaced with the "Gregorian" calendar in Great Britain and its American colonies. The Julian calendar was 11 days behind, so 14th September followed 2nd September on the day of the change. The days between the 3rd and 13th September, 1752, never happened.**

A mining hole in the mountains of Bohemia produced so much silver it became the official source of coinage for the entire Holy Roman Empire. The mine was in a valley called Joachimsthal, and the coins came to have the same name: "Joachimstalers." Over time this became shortened to "Talers" and over more time, the American pronunciation of the word became "Dollars".

**A fresh egg will sink in water; a stale one will float.**

**It is impossible to drown and not die. Technically the term "drowning" refers to the process of taking water into the lungs, not to death caused by that process.**

France and the United States are the only two teams to have entered all the World Cup soccer tournaments since 1936.

**A square mile of Amazon jungle can contain 3,000 different species of tree.**

In his final years, Emperor Napoleon was exiled to the tiny island of St Helena in the Atlantic. The wallpaper in his room was dyed with Scheele's Green, a colouring pigment that contained copper arsenite. When this wallpaper became damp, the mould converted the copper arsenite to a poisonous vapour form of arsenic. Napoleon died of arsenic poisoning. He was killed by his own wallpaper.

**The first James Bond movie, "Dr No", was released in 1963. Since then, the equivalent of half the world's population have seen at least one Bond movie.**

The number "007" originated in the 16th century. Bond author Ian Fleming based his character on Dr John Dee, the first British secret agent. Dee, who lived from 1527 to 1608, was an advisor to Queen Elizabeth I. He was a brilliant mathematician, magician, philosopher, alchemist and astrologer. At the time, England was at war with Spain, and, fearing spies, Dee used the 007 code for his letters to the Queen. The two zeros meant "for your eyes only".

**Mosquitoes prefer biting children to adults, and blondes to brunettes.**

# Did you know...

...that in times of hunger, Stone Age tribes would eat the old women before they ate their dogs?

The Bible has been translated into Klingon, the fictional language from Star Trek.

**There is a sport called "purring" which enjoys popularity in Wales.**
**The two opponents stand face-to-face, grasping each other firmly by the shoulders. At the starting signal, they begin kicking each other in the shins with shoes reinforced with metal toeplates. The first man to release his grip on his opponent's shoulders is the loser.**

The term "honeymoon" is a translation of a word coined by the Babylonians, who declared mead, a honey-flavoured wine, the official wedding drink, stating that the bride's parents be required to keep the groom supplied with the drink for one month following the wedding.

**The British royal family changed their surname from the German Saxe-Coburg-Gotha to Windsor in 1917. World War One broke out in 1914 and was in full fury in 1917. In protest, King George V renounced all the German titles belonging to him and his family and adopted the name of one of his castles, Windsor.**

On January 7th, 2002, Bob Bowling of Willard, Kentucky shot himself in the thigh while practising his quick draw on a snowman.

**In 1943, all American bakers were ordered to stop selling sliced bread for the duration of World War II. Only whole loaves were allowed to be sold to the public. It was never explained how this action helped the war effort in the slightest.**

Kissing under the mistletoe is a peculiarly British tradition. A girl is not supposed to refuse anyone a kiss beneath a sprig of mistletoe, even if it's someone really grim. Any boy who receives a kiss must pick a berry from the branch, and when all the berries have gone, no more **snogging is allowed.**

The fastest goal ever scored in a World Cup Finals tournament was netted by England captain Bryan Robson in 27 seconds against France in 1982. If he'd carried on scoring at that rate, England would have won 200 - nil.

**The car was invented by Karl Benz in 1885. Today, a new car is made every minute, every single day.**

If Stone Age people weren't feeling well, they would cut holes in each other with a sharp stone to let the pain escape.

**The ancient Romans had shows called Pantomimes hundreds of years ago. A man would read out a story, while silent actors played the parts behind him. Nobody dressed as a cow.**

A Flemish artist is responsible for the world's smallest paintings in history, including a picture of a miller and his mill, painted on a grain of corn.

**As far back as the 6th Century, it was customary to congratulate people who sneezed because it was thought that they were expelling evil from their bodies. During the great plague of Europe, the Pope at the time made it law to say "God bless you" to anyone who sneezed.**

A "coward" was originally a boy who took care of cows.

A person who collects postcards is called a "deltiologist".

Every minute 47 bibles are sold or distributed throughout the world.

In the 40's, the name of Bich pen was changed to Bic for fear that Americans would pronounce it "Bitch".

The word MAFIA stands for "Morte Alla Francia Italia Anela" or "Death to the French is Italy's Cry".

More people speak English in China than in the United States of America.

No word in the English language rhymes with month, orange, silver or purple.

People didn't always say "Hello" when they answered the phone. When the first regular phone service was established in 1878, people said "Ahoy-hoy".

Professional ballerinas can get through a dozen pairs of dancing shoes every week.

Ancient Anglo-Saxons celebrated the return of spring (Eostre) with a carnival. The party offerings, rabbits and coloured eggs, bid an end to winter. This festival occurred at the same time of year as the Christian observance of the Resurrection of Christ. Christian missionaries converted the Anglo-Saxons in the 2nd century, and the offering of rabbits and eggs eventually became the Easter bunny and Easter eggs.

Four US presidents have been assassinated: Abraham Lincoln in 1865, James A. Garfield in 1881, William H. McKinley in 1901, and John F. Kennedy in 1963.

**A seagull can drink seawater because it has special glands that filter out the salt.**

Charles VI, called "Charles the Mad", ruled France from 1380 to 1415. He believed that he was made of glass and put iron rods into his clothes to stop himself from breaking.

**There are now more than 6 billion human beings on Earth. According to the United Nations, the 6 billion mark was reached on October 12th, 1999.**

In ancient folklore, it was said that however hard they might try, witches can't say the Lord's Prayer.

OUR FARMER, WHO ART IN DEVON ...DOH! HAROLD BE THY NAME, VIKING DONE COME...

=SIGH!=

The nursery rhyme "Ring-a-ring of Roses" is a rhyme about the Plague. People infected with the Plague would get red circular sores (a ring of roses). These sores would smell quite horrible, so common folk would hide flowers on their bodies somewhere to cover the pong ("a pocket full of poseys"). People who died from the Plague would be burned so as to reduce the possible spread of the disease (originally "atishoo, atishoo... we all fall down").

**To melt away one pound of fat you would need to walk 34 miles.**

Ocean waves can travel as fast as a jet aeroplane.

**The Hawaiian alphabet has only 12 letters.**

In the middle of the Atlantic two of the huge plates that make the Earth's surface - the African Plate and the American plate - are moving apart at about the same speed as your fingernails grow.

**Every cubic mile of seawater holds over 150 million tons of minerals.**

In 1978, Emilio Marco Palma became the first person ever to be born in Antarctica.

**Before 1957, there was a law prohibiting any building in the city of Los Angeles having more than 13 storeys, as builders were afraid of earthquakes. Modern tall buildings in LA are "quake protected".**

London Bridge, built about 160 years ago, was bought and transported in 1968 to Lake Havasu, Arizona.

Several million trees every year grow as a result of squirrels forgetting where they buried their nuts.

All names originating from Hebrew that end with the letters el have something to do with God.

**The grand jury in America used to write "ignoramus" (meaning "we don't know" in Latin) on the back of verdicts that were undecided, or not to be sent to court. This was often an indication of the stupidity of the jury, hence its present meaning.**

In English, four is the only number that has the same number of letters

as its value.

**Naked means to be unprotected. Nude means unclothed.**

The teeth of a lobster are in its stomach.

**Traffic lights were used before the invention of the car. In 1868, a lantern with red and green signals was used at a London crossroads to control the flow of horse-drawn carriages and pedestrians.**

The first programme on American television was a Felix The Cat cartoon.

**The 33rd American president was named Harry S. Truman. His parents were going to give him the name Shippe or Solomon, the names of his grandfathers, but they could not agree on which, so they gave him just the initial "S".**

It is a 7,000,000,000-mile round-trip to the planet Pluto.

Grasshoppers have learned to hear with their legs, waving them in the air like little TV aerials feeling for sound waves.

**Some centipedes really do have 100 legs. The most legs a Pill Millipede has is 38.**

Athena Onassis Roussels is the granddaughter of a rich ship owner. When she was three years old, she inherited five billion dollars and her own Greek island. When she reaches the age of 18 in 2003, she can do what she likes with it.

**The American Government has 7.43 billion grams of gold in reserves. It is worth about 100,000,000,000 dollars (62.5 billion pounds sterling).**

America's first President, George Washington, had false teeth made of wood.

**"Corduroy" comes from the French, "Cord du Roi" or "cloth of the king".**

Forget-me-not: according to German legend this flower gets its name from the last words of a knight, who was drowned while trying to pick some from the riverside for his lady love.

**The most abundant bird on Earth is the Red-billed Quelea, a type of East African weaverbird. There are an estimated 1.5 billion adults in existence.**

The Antpitta avis canis Ridgley is a bird that looks like a stuffed duck on stilts and barks like a dog. The bird was discovered in Ecuador in June 1998. It is one of the largest new bird species discovered in recent centuries.

# Did you know...

...that some trains in Japan can reach speeds of up to 345 miles per hour?

Elephants can't jump.

**It's impossible to sneeze with your eyes open.**

Winston Churchill was born in a ladies' toilet during a dance.

**Not all our taste buds are on our tongue; some are on the roof of the mouth and in the cheeks.**

In Paris, the McDonalds big 'M' is the only one in the world that is white, rather than yellow. It was thought that yellow was too ugly.

**Fleas can accelerate 50 times faster than the space shuttle.**

It is forbidden for aircraft to fly over the Taj Mahal in India.

**The San Diego Zoo in California has the largest collection of animals in the world.**

The term "the Bogey man will get you" comes from the Boogy people who still inhabit an area of Indonesia. These people still act as pirates today and attack ships that pass.

**The world's biggest ice cream bar was made in Kalisz, Poland. In September of 1994, it took 11 days to make the bar which weighed 19,357 pounds when it was finished.**

Your heart beats 101,000 times a day. During your lifetime it will beat about three billion times and pump about 400 million litres (800 million pints) of blood.

At a steady jogger's pace of six miles per hour, it would take 173 days to jog around the Earth.

## Over 50 billion aspirins are taken worldwide each year.

The waters around Australia are home to more than half of the shark species in the world.

## Bamboo can grow three feet in a day.

Banging your head against a wall can burn up to 150 calories per hour.

## By age 65, the average person has spent nine years watching TV.

The height of the Eiffel Tower varies as much as six inches depending on the temperature.

## For every person on Earth, there are 200 million insects.

In one fateful operation of the early 1840s, one surgeon killed three people, including the patient, at one stroke. Before the days of anaesthetics, surgery was so painful, the finest surgeons were the fastest ones. In the 1840s, one of the best surgeons in England was Robert Liston. He boasted that he could amputate (chop off) a limb in less than two and a half minutes. One day, in his eagerness to amputate a leg in record time, he cut off another part of the patient's body and two of his assistants' fingers by mistake. The patient and the assistant died shortly afterwards. But an onlooker was so shocked at this catastrophe, he had a heart attack and died on the spot.

**The first thing ever cooked in a microwave oven was popcorn.**

The Christmas traditions of gift-giving and spicy mince pies both commemorate the Three Wise Men coming from the East.

**"I am" is the shortest complete sentence in the English language.**

The world's first stone lighthouse was the Smeaton Eddystone, built south of Plymouth in 1756. It was lit with only 24 candles. Today, lighthouses have the light-producing power of 20 million candles.

**Plant-eating dinosaurs did not eat grass, because there wasn't any. When the dinosaurs lived, trees and shrubs dominated the landscape. Flowering plants and grass evolved later.**

The slang word "crap" comes from Mr Thomas Crapper, the man who invented parts of the modern lavatory.

**A one-minute kiss burns 26 calories.**

The man featured on the American ten-dollar bill is Alexander Hamilton, a revolutionary war hero and leading architect of the first American government. He was killed in a duel on July 11th, 1804 by the American Vice-President, Aaron Burr.

**There are about 5,000 different languages spoken on Earth.**

The 1990s were the warmest decade in a thousand years. In this millennium, global temperature will increase between 3 and 6 degrees.

If you enjoyed this book, you can find more hilarious jokes, amazing facts, and brainbusting riddles and puzzles in the following books, also published by Dean:

| Title | ISBN |
|---|---|
| The World's Funniest Animal Jokes for Kids | 0 603 56064 4 |
| The World's Funniest Disgusting Jokes for Kids | 0 603 56065 2 |
| The World's Funniest School Jokes for Kids | 0 603 56063 6 |
| The World's Most Amazing Animal Facts for Kids | 0 603 56060 1 |
| The World's Most Amazing Planet Earth Facts for Kids | 0 603 56062 8 |
| The World's Most Amazing Science Facts for Kids | 0 603 56061X |
| 1000 of the World's Funniest Jokes for Kids | 0 603 56066 0 |
| 1000 of the World's Greatest Brainbusters | 0 603 56068 7 |

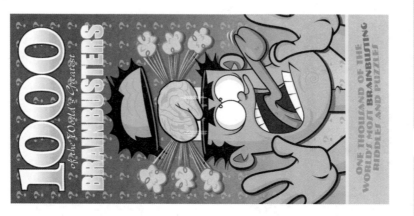

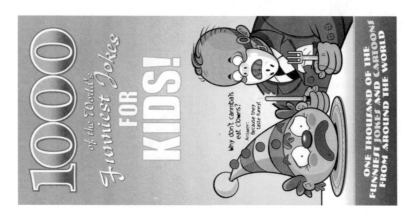